EDITOR: LEE JOHNSON

OSPREY MILITARY **WARRIOR SERIES** 15

LATE ROMAN CAVALRYMAN
236–565AD

Text by
SIMON MACDOWALL
Colour plates by
CHRISTA HOOK

First published in Great Britain in 1995 by
Osprey, an imprint of Reed Consumer Books Ltd.
Michelin House, 81 Fulham Road,
London SW3 6RB
and Auckland, Melbourne, Singapore and Toronto

ISBN 1 85532 567 5

Filmset in Great Britain
Printed through World Print Ltd, Hong Kong

Acknowledgements
Many thanks again to Bernd Lehnhoff for his many
contributions and also to Theodore Adamakopolous,
Stephen Allen, David Blanchard, Perry Gray, Kent
Haryett and Ross Macfarlane who have helped shape
my ideas over the years.

Dedication
To my parents with thanks for encouragement at an
early stage.

Artist's note
Readers may care to note that the original paintings
from which the colour plates in this book were pre-
pared are available for private sale. All reproduction
copyright whatsoever is retained by the publisher.
All enquiries should be addressed to:

> Scorpio Gallery
> P.O. Box 475
> Hailsham
> East Sussex
> BN27 2SL

The publishers regret that they can enter into no
correspondence upon the matter.

Publisher's Note
Readers may wish to study this title in conjunction with
the following Osprey publications:

> Warrior 9 *Late Roman Infantryman 236–565 AD*
> Elite 50 *The Praetorian Guard*
> MAA 46 *Roman Army (1) Caesar-Trajan*
> MAA 93 *Roman Army (2) Hadrian-Constantine*

If you would like to receive more information about
Osprey Military books, The Osprey Messenger is a
regular newsletter which contains articles, new title
information and special offers. To join free of charge
please write to:

**Osprey Military Messenger,
PO Box 5, Rushden,
Northants NN10 6YX**

LATE ROMAN CAVALRY

HISTORICAL BACKGROUND

The twilight of the Roman Empire saw a revolution in the way war was waged. The drilled infantryman, who had been the mainstay of Mediterranean armies since the days of the Greek hoplite, was gradually replaced by the mounted warrior. This change did not take place overnight, and in the 3rd and 4th centuries the role of the cavalryman was primarily to support the infantry. However, by the time of Justinian's reconquest of the west, in the 6th century, the situation had been completely reversed, and it was the infantryman who found himself in the supporting role.

The *eques*, or ordinary cavalryman, was in many ways similar to his infantry counterpart. He was more likely to have been a German, Sarmatian or Hun than an Italian, and he had probably never seen Rome. He fought for pay or booty, and did not particularly feel any great loyalty or sense of duty to the empire he was defending. Unlike the infantryman, however, he formed the elite of the army, and as time progressed his equipment and status improved as that of the infantryman declined. He was the precursor of the medieval knight who was to rule the battlefield for centuries to come.

Cavalry reserve of the 3rd century

The 3rd century AD was a period of chaos. Civil war and economic decline had greatly weakened the Empire, at a time of increasing pressure on the frontiers. Previously the Empire had been defended primarily by infantry-based armies protecting the *limes*, or frontier zones. The problem with this system was that when the frontier defences were penetrated, as happened with increasing frequency in the 3rd century, there were no troops in reserve to deal with the invasion. Another problem was that such break-

For centuries infantry had played the central role in Roman armies, with cavalry supporting them. Over the course of the late Roman period the importance of cavalry grew, and eventually it was the horseman who became the central figure in Roman armies. (Antonius Pius relief, 2nd century AD)

Modern reconstruction with 3rd-century equipment. The man on the left is wearing a panoply of fine bronze scales based on the Battle of Ebenezer fresco from Dura Europos in Syria. Similar hooded armour is depicted in the 4th-century Vergilus Vaticanus manuscript, and may have been worn in the eastern frontier regions. The man on the right is wearing more conventional equipment, representative of western cavalry units. (Author's photo)

throughs were often by fairly small, fast-moving bands of raiders (particularly the Goths along the Danube and the Franks and Alamanni along the Rhine): by the time temporary task forces, or *vexillationes*, had been drawn from the frontier defences and dispatched to the troubled areas, their foes had long since moved on.

One of the results of this pressure on the Empire's defensive system was an increase in the cavalry arm. This was not because cavalry had proved themselves tactically superior to infantry, but rather because fast-moving cavalry had a better chance of deploying quickly to trouble-spots. The emperor Gallienus (253–68) took this one step further and created all-cavalry reserve forces, which were based at strategic locations in northern Italy, Greece and the Balkans.

These reserves were probably created by withdrawing the old 120-man cavalry detachments from the legions and brigading them into new units called *equites promoti*. These in turn were supplemented by light skirmishers recruited in Illyricum (*equites dalmatae*) and North Africa (*equites mauri*), possibly together with heavier units of *equites scutarii*. Eventually these new units came to be collectively referred to as *equites illyriciani* or as *vexillatio*, a term which had originally meant a detachment drawn from the

frontier legions. The new *vexillationes* also enjoyed higher status than the old auxiliary cavalry. A unit at full strength was about 500 men.

The central cavalry reserve was instrumental in the success of the Illyrian emperors (Claudius, Aurelian, Probus, Carus and Diocletian) in restoring order in the latter part of the 3rd century. However, in the relative calm of Diocletian's reign (284–305) there was a partial return to a forward defensive strategy along the frontiers. Diocletian probably maintained a small central field army (*comitatus*) which included two *vexillationes* (*promoti* and *comites*) and three legions (*lanciarii, ioviani* and *herculiani*), but the bulk of the *equites illyriciani* were distributed along the eastern frontiers, and never quite regained their former status.

Reorganisation in the 4th century

The 4th century saw a complete reorganisation of the army. Constantine enlarged the *comitatus* to include five cavalry *vexillationes*, five legions and ten new small infantry units called *auxilia*. The *comitatus* were given higher status and privileges than the static frontier forces. In keeping with a trend that had been established by Gallienus in the mid-3rd century and reflecting the increasing importance of their role, the cavalry were ranked as senior to the legions and *auxilia*. Constantine also disbanded the Praetorian Guard and replaced it with the *scholae*, an all-cavalry force which included units of *scutarii* and *gentiles*.

A single centralised field army could not, however, cope with the frequent emergencies that erupted simultaneously at various points throughout the Empire. Constantine's successors, therefore, increased and divided up the *comitatus* to form several regional field armies (*comitatenses*) to act as reserves in Gaul, Illyricum, Thrace and the east, and gave a new designation (*palatini*) to the units of the emperor's central field army. Before long, units of *comitatenses* and *palatini* became mixed in the same armies, although the *palatini* continued to have higher status.

At some point the field army was split between the eastern and western halves of the Empire. This probably occurred in 365, when the Empire was divided between Valentinian and Valens. Many units were divided in two, keeping their original names but adding the designation *seniores* or *iuniores* to distinguish between them. It is quite possible that the two halves of a unit were not each recruited back up to their former strength but remained at a strength of about 300 – a unit size which carried through into Byzantine times.

We have a fairly good idea of how the army was organised from the *Notitia Dignitatum*, a contemporary document which lists all units at the end of the 4th century for the west and the beginning of the 5th century for the east. Several different types of cavalry are listed in this document, and in many cases we can deduce their role and equipment from the unit name. Units of *mauri*, *dalmatae* and *cetrati* were probably light, fast-moving javelin-armed skirmishers. The

Captured Sarmatian arms and equipment from the base of Trajan's Column. From the 2nd century onwards the Sarmatians heavily influenced the development and equipment of Roman cavalry. (Deutsche Archaologische Institut, Rome)

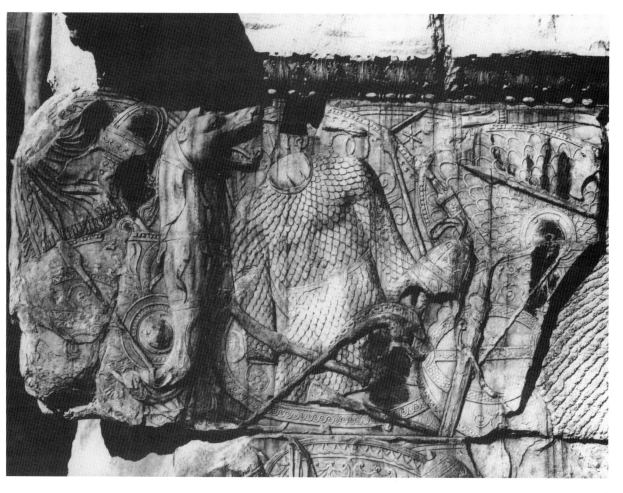

On campaign, cavalrymen played an important role scouting ahead of the army and screening its movements. When deployed on such duties, equipment and armour would be kept to a minimum for speed and stealth. (Arch of Constantine, Deutsche Archaologishe Institut, Rome)

many *equites sogittarii*, or horse archers, were probably also light cavalry, although some, such as the *Sagittarii Clibanarii*, would have been heavily equipped. Fully armoured lancers, modelled on Sarmatian, Parthian and Palmyran lancers, also formed part of the 4th-century army and were called *catafractarii* or *clibanarii*.

The majority of cavalry, however, were probably little different from the auxiliary cavalry of the earlier Empire, and were trained and equipped for close combat and for skirmishing from a distance with javelins. Such conventional heavy cavalry probably included units styled as *promoti*, *scutarii*, *stablesiani*, *armigeri*, *brachiati* and *cornuti* as well as those bearing Germanic or Gallic tribal names or named after reigning emperors. A few senior cavalry units were *comites* rather than *equites*, and some of these were further distinguished by a descriptive name (*Comites Alani* or *Comites clibanarii*, for example); the title was probably honorific.

All of these cavalry types could be found in the static frontier forces (*limitanei* and *ripenses*) as well as in the field armies. Some were the descendants of the old auxiliary *alae*; others included *illyriciani*, conventional *equites*, *catafractarii* and *sagittarii*. These were further supplemented by 'native' cavalry or *equites indigenae*, of which both *sagittarii* and *promoti* are recorded on the eastern frontier. Elsewhere, particularly on the Danube frontier, could be found units called *cunei equitum*, who may also have been semi-irregular, locally recruited cavalry.

Armies of the warlords

The aftermath of the disastrous Persian and Gothic campaigns of 363 and 378 respectively saw another change in the organisation of the Roman army. Heavy losses resulted in the transfer of many units of *limitanei* to the *comitatus* (where they were given the title of *psuedocomitatenses*). This probably resulted in a weakening of the frontier defences as well as a degradation in the quality of the field army. Roman commanders turned more and more to bands of barbarians to fill the ranks of their mobile field forces. Theodosius, for example, is reported to have employed 20,000 Goths at the battle of Figidus in AD 394. These barbarian allies (*foederati*) were given land to settle in return for military service; however, they fought together under their own leaders and were only nominally Romanised.

Increasingly, as the reliability of the regular field armies decreased, military commanders and even wealthy individuals began to hire bands of private retainers or *bucellarii*. The great warlords of the 5th century, such as Stilicho, Aetius and Aspar, all maintained large personal followings and came to rely on them almost exclusively. In AD 444 Valerian, a wealthy magnate in the east, is recorded as overpowering the local governor with a 'great horde of barbarians', and in the 6th century Belisarius employed as many as 7,000 *bucellarii*. Attempts were made to limit such private armies, including a law of AD 476 which made it illegal for individuals to maintain 'gangs of armed slaves, *bucellarii* or Isaurians'. However, it seems that the practice remained fairly common.

By the 6th century the *bucellarii* had been institutionalised and Roman field armies had evolved into large followings of mounted warriors who owed allegiance to powerful warlords – direct ancestors of the

feudal host. The old *comitatenses* were reduced, like the *limitanei*, to static garrisons, and the cavalry had become the arm of decision. Weapons too had changed: the typical Roman cavalryman now carried a bow as his principal weapon (probably as a result of Hunnic and Persian influences). Shock cavalry was provided primarily by the German *foederati*, who by the mid-6th century had evolved into regular units of lancers.

CHRONOLOGY

Major Battles in **bold**

236–268 Franks, Alamanni and Goths overrun Rhine and Danube frontiers.

251 Roman army defeated by Goths at **Forum Terebronii**.

258–261 Persian War. Romans defeated at **Edessa**; Emperor Valerian captured.

253–268 Reign of Gallienus. Creation of a central cavalry reserve.

268–280 Illyrian emperors restore the frontiers.

271–273 Aurelian's successful campaign against Palmyra.

Hadrian's Wall, the most famous of Rome's frontier defences. The frontier zones were manned by static garrison troops known as limitanei. *(English Heritage)*

284–305 Reign of Diocletian. Complete reorganisation of imperial administration.

312 Constantine defeats Maxentius at **Milvan Bridge**.

313 Edict of Milan brings recognition for Christianity.

324–337 Constantine sole emperor. Construction of new capital at Byzantium (Constantinople).

337–350 Inconclusive war with Persia.

351 Constantius' eastern army defeats the western troops of the usurper Magnentius at **Mursa**.

355–360 Julian's successful campaign against the Franks and Alamanni in Gaul.

357 Roman victory over the Alamanni at **Strasbourg**.

363 Failed campaign against the Persians.

368–369 'Barbarian conspiracy' of Saxons, Picts and Scots overrun Britain; order restored by Theodosius.

378 East Roman army destroyed by Goths at **Adrianople**; Emperor Valens killed.

Sarmatian cataphracts from Trajan's Column. These formed the model for the equites cataphractarii *introduced into the Roman army in the 2nd century, probably recruited from Sarmatian settlers in Gaul. The skin-tight suits of scale armour are a flight of fancy on the part of the artist. (Deutsche Archaologische Institut, Rome)*

379–395	Reign of Theodosius. Some semblance of order restored.
394	Theodosius' eastern army, including 20,000 Goths, defeats the western army of Arbogast at **Frigid River**.
401–404	Inconclusive campaign of Stilicho against Alaric.
405–406	Vast German migration led by Radagaisus defeated by Stilicho at **Florence**.
406–410	Vandals, Suevi, Alans and Burgundians cross the frozen Rhine and overrun Gaul and Spain.
407	Roman troops leave Britain.
410	Alaric sacks Rome.
419	Visigoths establish independent kingdom in southern Gaul.
421–422	Moderately successful campaign against Persia.
429	Vandals and Alans cross from Spain into Africa.
431	Failed joint east-west Roman campaign against Vandals in Africa.
433–450	Campaigns of Aetius against Visigoths, Franks and Burgundians in Gaul.
441–443	Hun invasion of the east. Romans defeated in the **Chersonese Peninsula**; Balkans ravaged. Romans agree to pay tribute.
447	Second Hunnic invasion of the east bought off by the Romans.
451	Hun invasion of the west checked by Aetius at **Chalons**.
455	Vandal sack of Rome.
476	Italian field army overthrows Emperor Romulus Augustulus. End of western empire.
492–496	Isaurian War. Primarily Gothic army under Anastasius defeats Isurian partisans of Longinus.
507–512	Anastasius fortifies the frontiers against the Persians and Slavs.
524–531	Justinian's first war with Persia; ends inconclusively.
532	Nika riots in Constantinople; 30,000 people die before order is restored.
533–534	East Romans under Belisarius recover Africa from the Vandals.
534–554	Gothic War. A devastated Italy restored to the Empire.
539–562	Justinian's second Persian War; typically inconclusive.

CONDITIONS OF SERVICE

Recruitment

In many ways recruitment was similar to that of the infantry. The military profession, like others, was partly hereditary: sons of soldiers and veterans, including officers, were expected to serve unless physically unfit. There were some volunteers, particularly from Germans living outside the Empire, and sometimes bounties were offered to attract them. However, military service was very unpopular, and hereditary and voluntary enlistment were not enough to fill the ranks, so many soldiers were levied by conscription.

As the elite of the army, the cavalry were better paid, had higher social status and led a better life than the infantry, and as such would have had the pick of recruits. According to the 5th-century writer Flavius Vegetius Renatus, promotion to the cavalry was through the infantry ranks, but other methods of entry were also possible. Laws from AD 326 state that 'Sons of veteran cavalrymen can go straight into the cavalry if they have a horse' and 'If any son of a veteran shall have two horses, or a slave and a horse, he shall serve in the rank of *circitor* [the lowest non-commissioned rank]'. Presumably other recruits of higher social standing or with riding experience might also have been able to get into the cavalry without being sons of veterans. Barbarian recruits from areas noted for their horsemanship, or who brought their own horses, were probably also considered.

The traditional recruitment system seems to have broken down in the 5th century. Although the recruitment of individuals continued, it became increasingly common for Roman armies to hire whole bands of barbarians in return for money or land to settle. Powerful warlords would recruit their own private armies, and use them to further their own causes or hire them out to the government. These private retainers, or *bucellarii*, became the mainstay of 5th- and early 6th-century armies. They were exclusively cavalrymen, and could be recruited from the tough frontier areas of the Empire or from outside barbarians. In the 5th century most would have been Germans or Huns; in the 6th century Procopius mentions Armenians, Cilicians, Cappadocians, Pisidians, Isuarians, Thracians, Huns and Persians. The *Strategikon* recommends that units be formed of a mixture of veterans and recruits, 'otherwise the older men, if formed by themselves, may be weak, and the younger, inexperienced men may turn out disorganised'.

In the east, after the fall of the western empire, recruitment again became centralised and seems, surprisingly, to have become entirely voluntary. The Justinian Code makes no reference to hereditary enlistment or conscription. The static units of *limitanei* (and *comitatenses*, who had become static by the 6th century) were recruited locally. Men volun-

We do not know much about shield designs from the 3rd century, but finds from Dura Europos indicate that mythical scenes were popular. They could well have been individual designs painted on a background of a common unit colour. This conjectural reconstruction shows that the owner was a follower of Mithras, the most popular soldiers' religion until well into the Christian period. (Author's photo)

teered for these units knowing that they would not serve away from home and could pursue a fairly comfortable career, with opportunities to conduct other business. Volunteers for the field armies, which were quite small by earlier standards, could be found in the mountains of the Balkans and Asia Minor. For example, in AD 549 Germanus went on a recruiting campaign in the Balkans and 'by handing out, without stint, the large sums of money he had received from the emperor, and more from his own pocket, was able in a brief space to collect a surprisingly large army of good fighting men'.

Provision of horses

The individual soldier was only half of what was needed to make a cavalryman: larger numbers of horses than men were required to keep a cavalry unit operating. A Roman cavalry horse has been estimated to have had a useful life expectancy of about three to five years on active service. Animal casualties would probably have been higher than rider casualties, since not only is the horse a larger and easier target, but injuries, whether in combat or on long marches, would have been more likely to make it unusable for further service. A strong remount industry was essential, therefore, to keep mobile the relatively large number of cavalry in the late Roman army.

Some horses were provided by recruits themselves, and a few others might have been captured in battle, but this would only have accounted for a small fraction of the number required. In the 3rd and early 4th century remounts were collected as a levy on provincials and were drafted into the army in much the same way as a conscript. A law of AD 369, for example, states that a *comes* (count) had to supply three horses every five years. Before long this levy was commuted into a cash tax. Another law of AD 369 states that persons subject to the tax were to pay 23

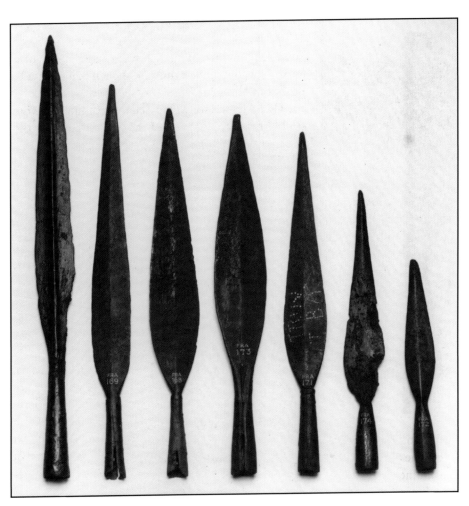

A selection of Roman spear-heads. Cavalry spears were usually fairly light, and could be thrown or kept in the hand for close combat. (National Museum of Scotland)

A close-up view of the spangenhelm-style helmets worn by the Sarmatians on Trajan's Column. This helmet style spread from the Danube regions throughout the Roman and Germanic world to become the most popular helmet type. (Deutsche Archaologische Institut, Rome)

Below: A similar close-up of Roman spangenhelms being worn two centuries later by soldiers on the Arch of Galerius. (Deutsche Archaologische Institut, Rome)

end of the 4th century soldiers were given 7 *solidi* to buy their mounts. If this was the actual price of a horse, the government must have been making a tidy profit out of the tax.

Other horses were obtained by breeding, on large stud farms. Perhaps some of the cash obtained by the horse tax went to offset the cost of running them. A good cavalry horse who had been injured or was too old for military service could still have many years producing offspring for the army.

The Romans' criteria for a suitable horse is not known. Laws from the mid-4th century state that 'horses shall meet certain requirements as to shape, stature and age', but unfortunately these standards are not specified. There was certainly room for corruption on the part of the *comes stabuli* and other officials: the temptation to collect taxes in full and then purchase inferior cheaper horses and pocket the difference must have been great. Ammianus Marcellinus, writing in the 4th century, tells us: 'Constantin, a riding master, who had been sent to Sardinia to inspect cavalry mounts, took the liberty of exchanging a few of them and was stoned to death at Valentinian's command.' Ammianus uses this as an example of Valentinian's cruelty, implying that low-level corruption was normal, and unofficially accepted.

solidi per horse and that cash was to be paid rather than horses. From this money the *comes stabuli*, whose job it was to collect and examine horses for the government, drew a fee of 2 *solidi* per horse. At the

TRAINING

'Constant drill is of the greatest value to the soldier,' says the *Strategikon*, and training in the cavalry seems to have been fairly rigorous throughout this period. While Vegetius complains that training and discipline in the infantry had greatly declined by the 5th century, he implies that in the cavalry it had improved.

Training a cavalryman had always been more complex than training an infantryman, since in addition to learning basic soldierly skills, a good cavalryman needed to form a real partnership with his mount, which in turn had to be trained as a war horse. The practice of recruiting cavalrymen by promotion from the infantry, in which case the new cavalryman would already be a skilled soldier, or from men who owned a horse, which meant they had riding skills, made sense. What remained was to bring soldierly skills and horsemanship together.

The new cavalryman had to learn and perfect weapons-handling skills using swords, javelins and light lances while both mounted and dismounted, and from the mid-5th century archery also became a required skill. The *Strategikon*, for example, tells us that the soldier should 'shoot rapidly mounted on his horse at a run, to the front, the rear, the right and the left'. Learning to mount and dismount quickly (without the aid of stirrups) was also practised. Arrian, in his *Tactica*, written just before this period, says that skilled cavalrymen would demonstrate 'how a man wearing armour can leap on to his horse when it is running'. A few centuries later Vegetius recom-

mends setting up wooden horses and teaching recruits to 'vault on them at first without arms, afterwards completely armed'. He goes on to say:

'Such was their attention to this exercise that they were accustomed to mount and dismount on either side indifferently with their drawn swords or spears in their hands. By assiduous practice in the leisure of peace, their cavalry was brought to such perfection of discipline that they mounted their horses in an instant even amidst the confusion of sudden and unexpected alarms.'

After mastering the basic skills, the cavalryman would need to learn how to jump obstacles, ride over uneven terrain, and to execute circles, turns and fast

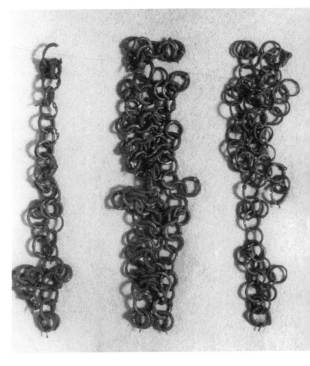

Above: Examples of Roman ring mail, the most common form of body armour for cavalrymen, particularly in the west. (National Museums of Scotland)

A close-up of Roman mail, showing its construction of alternating riveted and welded rings. (National Museums of Scotland)

12

tops. Vegetius tells us that the cavalry trained on 20-mile marches three times a month, practising their evolutions, pursuing, retreating and charging over varied terrain. Similar exercises in varied conditions and terrain are also recommended by the *Strategikon*:

'*It is essential that the horses become accustomed not only to rapid manoeuvring in open level country, but also over hilly, thick and rough ground and in quick ascending and descending of slopes . . . The men who spare their horses and neglect drills of this sort are really planning their own defeat. It is also a good idea for the troops to become used to doing this work in hot weather, for nobody really knows what situations may arise.*'

Once both horse and rider had been trained individually, they had to learn how to operate as part of a larger formation. In the *Tactica*, Arrian describes numerous complex manoeuvres, carried out by cavalry display teams, which mirrored the requirements of the battlefield and emphasised fluid skirmishing tactics. Arrian stresses the importance of standards in keeping units together while executing these rapid manoeuvres:

'*Standards do not merely provide the eye with a pleasurable thrill, but they also serve a useful purpose in keeping apart* [the units involved in] *the charge and preventing the ranks from tangling with each other. For*

those who bear them are the men most skilled in doubling back and wheeling, and when they choose to make continually new circles and one direct charge after another, the body of the troops only have to follow their own standards. Thus the succession of various kinds of wheeling, of manifold types of doubling back and of charging in different ways nevertheless causes no confusion in the ranks.'

The skills taught to 6th-century units are similar to those described by Arrian, and indicate that although weaponry had changed, basic unit drill had not. Drills including opening and closing ranks, charging, pursuing, turning and wheeling; as the following passage shows, cavalry manoeuvre remained fast and fluid.

'*If a single bandon* [unit of 300 men] *is to be drilled by itself, most of the men should be formed in extended order. On the same line with them about ten horsemen should be drawn up in single file on each flank in close order. A few other soldiers, about ten, should take their position on the opposite front to represent the enemy so our men can give the impression of directing their charge against them. When the advance begins, the troops in extended order separate from their close order support and move out rapidly as though for combat. After riding steadily forward for a mile or two, they then turn back*

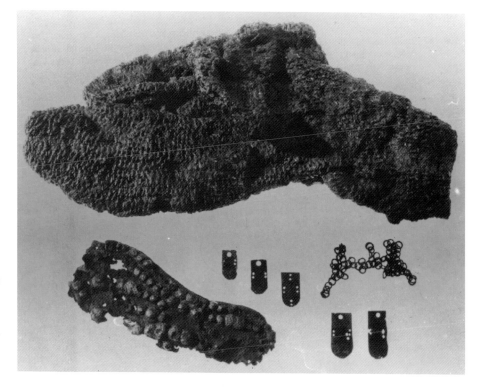

Equipment found in a Roman cavalry fort in Germany (Biriciana). Mail and scale have often been found in the same location, implying a lack of uniformity within units. Note the studs on the sole of the sandal. (Author's photo)

about half that distance, make three or four quick charges to the right and to the left, and then circle back again. After all this they gallop back to their original position in the area between the two close-order groups, and together with them they ride out as if to encounter a pursuing enemy.'

Conditions, pay and rations

The late Roman soldier was allowed to marry, and his family was usually maintained at public expense. Sons of soldiers (who were obliged to follow their father's footsteps) were entered on unit strength and drew rations. Although in AD 381 Libanius complained that soldiers were no longer receiving maintenance for their families, laws from the early 5th century detail ration allowances for soldiers' families.

In addition to maintaining a family, many soldiers had slaves or servants. The 6th-century *Strategikon* indicates that the use of servants by the soldiers had become formalised and that they had specific duties:

'Those men, especially those receiving allowances for the purpose, should certainly be required to provide servants for themselves, slave or free, according to regulations in force. At the time of distributing pay, care should be taken, just as with the soldiers, to register the servants and their arms . . . If some of the men are unable to afford servants, then it will be necessary to require three or four lower-ranking soldiers to join in maintaining one servant . . . There should be enough servants for each section to take care of their horses, in proportion to the differing rank of the units or the number of horses.'

We get glimpses of routine daily life for a cavalryman from surviving unit and personal records, mostly from Egypt and in the main describing duties carried out by static troops. The duties carried out by the *Ala Quinta Praelectorum*, a unit of Egyptian

A cavalry mêlée between Romans and Persians from the Arch of Galerius. Various wars with Persia dominated the late Roman period. (Deutsche Archaologische Institut, Rome)

Horse armour, because of its weight and expense, was probably quite rare. Examples of full scale horse armour have been found at Dura Europos, but their use was probably limited to the clibanarii of the eastern regions. Chamfrons like this one, although thought to be designed for cavalry games, may have been more widespread and used in combat by western cataphractarii. (National Museums of Scotland)

limitanei in the mid-4th century, include policing, routine patrolling, tax collecting and even providing nets to catch gazelles. The work of such static cavalry units in peaceful regions probably equates more to that of a modern border police than a regular military unit.

As time progressed these static units increasingly took on the appearance of part-time militias. Laws from the 5th century onwards indicate that many men of the *limitanei*, and later the *comitatenses* as well, took up other occupations. Many farmed their own land, others worked the land of powerful landowners, and some had private businesses. An order from the emperor Leo in the mid-5th century informs the patrician Aspar that soldiers should be occupied with public duties and not devote themselves to cultivating fields or looking after animals or to commerce.

They were in future not to be seconded to the service of private estates, and were supposed to remain with their units to drill each day. Despite official displeasure these practices continued. One soldier in 6th-century Alexandria is recorded as spending most of the day weaving baskets and praying, only joining his unit for military duties in the evening. Other records from Egypt show that many soldiers had extensive business dealings and openly carried out other occupations.

Soldiers in field army units, with no fixed base, would have had little opportunity for other occupations. This, however, was balanced by high status, better pay and plenty of opportunity for battlefield loot. The field army soldiers led a more dangerous life than their counterparts in static units, as they were far more likely to be called on for serious combat. They could also be posted from one end of the Empire to the other. Being moved far away from their home areas caused great resentment among the soldiers, even if they were allowed to bring their families. In AD 360, for example, the Gallic field army mutinied when faced with an order to move east to join a campaign against the Persians.

Field army soldiers were billeted on the local population and were given allowances to purchase food and other necessities. On campaign they might live under canvas and be supplied with hard rations, but this was not always the case. Describing the occupation of Carthage by Belisarius' troops, for example, Procopius tells us:

'The clerks drew up their lists of the men and conducted the soldiers to their lodgings as usual, and the soldiers themselves, getting their lunch by purchase from the market, rested as each one wished.'

EQUIPMENT

Issue and supply

In theory the soldier received his clothing and equipment from the state, but in the anarchic period of the 3rd century there was no centralised supply system. Soldiers were supposedly supplied from workshops attached to their fort, but many units, particularly cavalry, were almost constantly on duties elsewhere, and rarely saw their home base. Re-supply, therefore, would have had to come from a variety of sources: battlefield salvage, pillage, local purchase or official re-supply from locations other than the soldier's home base. The result would have been that rarely would two 3rd-century cavalrymen have looked alike, and might have had serious equipment deficiencies.

The creation of state-run arms factories (*fabricae*) at the end of the 3rd century may have been an attempt to find a better way of supplying soldiers who were constantly on the move. Even then, there was no concept of uniformity in the modern sense: *fabricae* continued to build on local traditions, so that a workshop in the east might produce scale armour while a similar one in the west produced mail. Since the field armies were mobile, individual soldiers in the same unit could wear a variety of styles of equipment, reflecting a variety of supply sources. The 4th-century soldier was probably better and more efficiently equipped than his 3rd-century predecessor, but except in static units he would still not have presented much of a uniform appearance.

Central re-supply began to break down again towards the end of the 4th century, and equipment issues were replaced by allowances from which the soldier was expected to equip himself. A law of AD 375, for example, states that recruits were to be given 6 *solidi* to buy clothing and for other initial expenses. By the 6th century even horses, weapons and armour were supplied in this way, although the powerful warlords of the 5th and 6th centuries sometimes supplied their retainers out of their own pockets. Procopius, for example, praises Belisarius' generosity in replacing arms and horses lost in battle by his men at his own expense.

An attempt at the end of the 6th century to replace the allowance system with uniform and arms issues caused great resentment in the army, which suggests firstly that soldiers did not spend their full allowances on equipping themselves, and further that equipment varied greatly between units and even within the same unit.

Basic clothing and equipment

The soldier's clothing, probably bought on the local market, would have reflected the civilian fashions of the time, and should not be thought of as 'uniform' in the modern sense. The basic dress was a very loose-fitting long-sleeved tunic decorated with contrasting coloured bands at the cuffs and neck, and discs on the shoulders and skirt. Most tunics would have been made of undyed wool, linen or a wool-linen mix, and they might have been bleached white or left a natural light beige. Wealthier soldiers, or those who wished to present a more military appearance, might have purchased red dyed tunics which had long been considered a military colour. Other colours – blue, green and yellow – were less common but are shown on some mosaics and paintings from the period.

Leg-wear varied according to the region and the season. In cold climates breeches or long trousers were worn, usually of dark brown wool, although some cavalrymen may have worn leather breeches. The lower legs were often covered by knee-high socks bound up with laces in a cross-garter pattern, or with wrap-around puttee-like bindings. In warmer climates the lower leg coverings were often worn without breeches or trousers.

To keep out the cold and wet, each soldier had a thick wool cloak, or *sagum*. Dull yellow or reddish browns seem to have been the most common cloak colours, but richer soldiers and officers might have worn brighter hues. When not in use, the cloak was rolled up behind the trooper's saddle. The *Strategikon* (a 6th-century military manual) states that soldiers' cloaks should be 'large enough to wear over their armaments' so as to protect them from dampness. It explained other benefits too: 'Such cloaks are also necessary in another way on patrol, for when the mail is covered by them, its brightness will not be seen at a distance by the enemy, and they also provide some protection against arrows.'

It was the soldier's equipment, not the colour or style of his clothing, that set him apart from his civilian counterpart. The most basic military item was a wide leather belt decorated with bronze stiffeners and studded with various straps and fasteners to allow the attachment of extra personal equipment such as a purse or knife. The long sword, or *spatha*, was worn on the left side, usually suspended from a baldric over the right shoulder, but it could also be worn from the waist-belt. Most cavalrymen

carried a spear, or *hasta*, as their primary offensive weapon, but they supplemented it with several light javelins which might be held in the left hand behind the shield or in a javelin case behind the saddle.

The shield

The most important piece of defensive equipment was the shield. This was the only part of their equipment where pains were taken to provide some degree of uniformity as a means of identification. The 5th-century writer Flavius Vegetius Renatus tells us that each unit had a distinctive shield emblem. This is substantiated by the *Notitia Dignitatum*, which lists the shield designs of most units at the end of the 4th century, and by later Byzantine manuals, which suggest that each unit should be identified by a common shield and colour of helmet plume. This does not imply that all men in the unit would have carried elaborately painted shields; after a battle, damaged shields would have had to be replaced from battlefield salvage or perhaps from a central reserve, and it is highly unlikely that a soldier on campaign would have had the time or the paint to reproduce some of the highly detailed de-

Right: Additional leg and arm defences, like this example from Scotland, would have been worn by Roman cataphracts. A unit of cataphractarii *was stationed in north Britain during this period. (National Museums of Scotland)*

Far right: A modern reconstruction of a laminated thigh guard. (National Museums of Scotland)

signs shown in the *Notitia* before his next engagement. At best, he might have managed a quick coat of paint in the official unit colour.

With the possible exception of some specialised skirmisher units, Roman cavalry wore some form of armour. The helmet was almost universal, although styles would vary greatly, even in the same unit. Monuments and gravestones from the 3rd century onwards tend to depict soldiers, whether infantry or cavalry, without armour. This has led many modern authors to believe that except for cataphracts, late Roman soldiers were unarmoured. Literary evidence, however, indicates that cavalry armour became more complete in the later Empire, and that the average trooper would have worn at least a light mail shirt similar to that of the auxiliary cavalry of earlier periods.

Cataphractarii and *clibanarii*

While most Roman cavalry performed almost a light cavalry role, some units were specially armed and equipped as shock cavalry. These had the generic name of cataphracts (*cataphractarii* or *cataphracti*). Their name stems from the word '*cataphracta*', which is repeatedly used by Vegitius to describe armour of any type, whether worn by infantry, cavalry or even elephants. Some of these heavily armoured units were also known as *clibanarii*. A description by Ammianus, for example, describes completely armoured lancers as '*cataphracti equites (quos clibanarios dictitant)*' – 'cataphract cavalry (which they call *clibanarii*)'. The fact that the terms *cataphractarii* and *clibanarii* were loosely and sometimes interchangeably applied by ancient writers has caused no end of confusion among modern scholars. Both types were clearly more heavily armoured than conventional cavalry, and any difference between the two most likely stems from their origins rather than their role.

Equites cataphractarii were first introduced in the Roman army by Hadrian in the 2nd century. They were modelled on the Sarmatians, and as such would have worn fairly complete scale coats and *spangenhelm* helmets, carried a long lance (*contus*) in two hands, and had no shield. The horses of these *cataphractarii* may or may not have been armoured. Some literary descriptions mention horse armour, others do not. Monuments are equally vague: Trajan's Column depicts Sarmatians riding elaborately armoured horses while later funeral *stelae* of members of the *Equites Cataphractarii Pictavenses* and *Equites Cataphractarii Ambianses* show armoured riders on unarmoured horses. One thing is clear, however, *cataphractarii* were more heavily armoured than conventional cavalry, and fought with a long lance rather than the traditional lighter spears and javelins.

When on campaign in hostile territory, soldiers of the field army would have lived in leather tents like this modern reconstruction. (Author's photo)

Soldiers of the limitanei lived in fixed bases along the frontier, like this fort at Chester which originally housed a cavalry unit. (English Heritage)

Many Sarmatians were settled in Gaul in return for military service, and it is interesting to note that most of the known *cataphractarii* units have Gallic- or Celtic-sounding names such as the *Biturigenses*, *Ambianenses*, *Albigenses* and *Pictavenses*. These names suggest that the *cataphractarii* can be linked back to the Sarmatian military settlers in Gaul.

The *clibanarii*, on the other hand, have Persian or Parthian origins, and were probably not introduced into the Roman army until the 4th century. Persian armoured cavalry and their Roman derivative inspired awe in 4th-century writers. Along with the detailed description of them as very heavily armoured lancers, this indicates that their armour was more complete and more impressive than that of the Sarmatian-style *equites cataphractarii* who had been around for centuries. The term '*clibanarius*' may derive from '*clibanus*', meaning 'baking oven' – an appropriate term for a heavily armoured man fighting in the hot climate of the Middle East. The men who fought in these units were probably of Persian or Middle Eastern origin, and their equipment would

have shown Persian rather than Sarmatian origins. While it is quite likely that *clibanarii* would have ridden horses covered with armoured trappings similar to those discovered at Dura Europos, several descriptions by Ammianus are notable in that they give great detail about the rider's armour but do not mention the horse's.

Clibanarii units were senior to *cataphractarii*. There was one unit in the *scola* (guards) and the remainder were *palatini* (cavalry of the central field army), while the *cataphractarii* units were either *comitatenses* or *limitanei*. This lends weight to the idea that *clibanarii* might have been a newer, more completely armoured, version of *cataphractarii*. It should also be noted that there were four *fabricae* devoted to producing *clibanaria*, so the *clibanarii* probably had some form of special armour.

One unit of *clibanarii* does not fit the contemporary descriptions of fully armoured lancers. This is the *Equites Sagittarii Clibanarii*, listed in the *Notitia*

Dignitatum as part of the North African field army. This unit may have been modelled on Persian armoured horse archer units, which by the 6th century had become the standard Roman cavalry type, but we have no way of knowing if they rode armoured horses. Some modern authors have taken the evidence of this one unit to suggest that all *clibanarii* were armed with bows and were lighter equipped than *cataphractarii*, but the fact that this unit is specifically designated as '*sagittarii*' indicates that it was an anomaly rather than the norm. Furthermore, contemporary descriptions of Roman *clibanarii* or Persian-style cataphracts usually have them as lancers.

Horse archers

Horse archers had always formed part of the Roman army's cavalry force, particularly in the east, but their importance increased greatly throughout this period. Although they were traditionally light skirmishers, probably without armour, at some point, probably in the 5th century, the standard Roman cavalryman evolved into an armoured horse archer capable of skirmishing from a distance or fighting in hand-to-hand combat. We have already discussed the possible Persian influence in the development of at least one unit of 4th-century armoured horse archers, and this, combined with influences from the steppe peoples such as the Huns, may have led to the transformation of the Roman cavalryman. It was probably a gradual process, and may have occurred between AD 430 and 450, when Aetius held power in the west and used large numbers of Huns in his army.

The armoured Roman horse archer of the 6th century who formed the basis of Belisarius' army is clearly described by Procopius:

'*The bowmen of the present time go into battle wearing corselets and fitted out with greaves which extend up to the knee. From the right side hang their arrows, from the other the sword. And there are some*

The destruction of the Praetorians by Constantine's cavalry at the Battle of Milvan Bridge. The scale armour for the Praetorians and *lack of armour for other troops was an artistic convention. (Deutsche Archaologische Institut, Rome)*

These very classical style Attic helmets worn by many troops on the Arch of Constantine were probably another artistic convention, although it is likely that a different style of Attic helmet was worn during the late Roman period, especially in Hellenistic regions. (Deutsche Archaologische Institut, Rome)

who have a spear also attached to them, and at the shoulders, a sort of small shield without a grip, such as to cover the region of the face and neck. They are expert horsemen, and are able without difficulty to direct their bows to either side while riding at full speed, and to shoot an opponent whether in pursuit or in flight.'

THE EXPERIENCE OF BATTLE

Skirmish tactics

Before the 5th century Roman commanders expected to win their battles with a decisive infantry clash. The cavalryman's job on the battlefield was to support the infantryman and to provide the circumstances that would allow the former to do his job. Most Roman cavalrymen fought using skirmish tactics, and although they might have worn armour, they could be considered as 'light cavalry'. On the march they might act as scouts, forage for food, lay enemy territory to waste or protect the flanks and rear of the column. When the army formed up for battle the cavalry would be called on to screen the deployment, hamper enemy deployment, protect the flanks of the infantry, defeat enemy cavalry and

pursue broken opponents. They were not expected to deliver the crushing blow that would defeat the enemy army; that was the job of the infantry.

The best surviving account of 3rd-century cavalry in action comes from Zosimus, who clearly describes the skirmish tactics employed by Aurelian's cavalry against Palmyran cataphracts in AD 272:

'He [Aurelian] ordered his cavalry not to engage immediately with the fresh cavalry of the Palmyrans, but to wait for their attack and pretend to flee, and to continue so doing until excessive heat and the weight of their armour had so wearied men and horses that they had to give up the chase. This stratagem worked, as the cavalry adhered to the order of the emperor. When they saw their enemy tired and that the horses were scarcely able to stand under them, or themselves to move, the Romans drew up the reins of their horses and, wheeling around, charged the enemy, trampling them as they fell from their horses. A confused slaughter ensued, some falling by the sword and others by their own and their enemies' horses.'

Zosimus goes on to describe the several follow-on engagements in which the infantry form the main battle line 'with shields close to each other and in compact formation' and named units of *equites illyriciani (dalmatae and mauri)* employ the same hit and run light cavalry tactics, but this time with less success:

'*At the commencement of the engagement, the Roman cavalry made a partial withdrawal, in case the Palmyrans, who outnumbered them and were better horsemen, should surround the Roman army unawares. But the Palmyran cavalry pursued them so fiercely, though their ranks were broken, that the outcome was quite contrary to the expectation of the Roman cavalry. For they were pursued by an enemy much superior in strength and therefore most of them fell. The infantry had to bear the brunt of the action. Observing that the Palmyrans had broken their ranks when the cavalry commenced their pursuit, they wheeled about and attacked them while they were scattered and in disarray.*'

Accounts of cavalry tactics from the 4th century

Roman horse harnesses were heavily decorated with gilded and silvered phalerae, fasteners and pendants. (National Museums of Scotland)

present a similar picture. Ammianus Marcellinus describes a cavalry action as 'not a pitched battle but a succession of quick skirmishes'. When the army deploys for battle it is still the infantry who are expected to form up in the centre to fight the main action – 'their flank covered by squadrons of cavalry'. This is how the Roman army deployed for the Battle of Strasbourg in AD 357 and at Adrianople in AD 378. Although the infantry were expected to bear the brunt of the heavy fighting, the success of the cavalry in protecting the flanks and defeating the enemy cavalry could decide the action. At Adrianople, for example, Ammianus tells us:

'*Our left wing penetrated as far as the Gothic wagons, and would have gone further if it had received any support, but it was abandoned by the rest of the cavalry, and under pressure of numbers gave way and collapsed like a broken dyke. This left the infantry unprotected.*'

Formations

According to Arrian:

'There are various formations of cavalry of many kinds, some square, some oblong, some rhombus-shaped, while others are brought together in a wedge. All these formations are good when adopted at the right time, and one would not pick out one of them and judge it superior to the others, since in another spot against different enemies and on a different occasion one might find another formation more useful than the one for which one had adopted.'

The wedge (and the rhomboid, a diamond-shaped formation) was particularly suited to fast skirmish action. With the leader and standard bearer at the point, command and control of the unit became simple, as all the troopers had to do was conform to the movement of the standard. These formations allowed 'the carrying out of sharp wheeling movements . . . for it is hard to wheel about with square formations'. Furthermore, as Vegetius tells us, a wedge 'pierces the enemy line by a multitude of darts directed to one particular place'. The cavalry wedge, therefore, was naturally a preferred formation of light horse archers such as the Scythians and Huns, and should not be confused with the Germanic wedge which was more like an attack column. (See Warrior 9, *Late Roman Infantryman*.)

The emperor surrounded by his guards, from the Arch of Constantine. After the destruction of the Praetorians at Milvan Bridge, Constantine created an all-cavalry guard known as the Schola. (Deutsche Archaologische Institut, Rome)

A Roman cavalryman hunting. The Strategikon recommends hunting as a form of training for the cavalry. The man's clothing – red tunic with purple decorative patches and bands; and knee socks bound with thin laces – is typical of the late Roman period. (Piazza Armerina, Sicily)

The square and oblong formations would be used when complicated manoeuvre was less important than the ability to deliver an effective charge. A square was usually four ranks deep. Arrian tells us:

'*Cavalry drawn up in depth do not afford the same assistance as do infantry in depth, for they do not push on those in front of them, since one horse cannot push against another in the way that infantry push on with their shoulders and flanks. Nor when they are contiguous with those drawn up in front do they constitute a single massed weight for the whole body of troops; on the contrary, if they mass and press against each other, they rather cause the horses to panic.*'

The author of the *Strategikon* made the same point, saying that four ranks was enough and that extra depth added nothing. However, he conceded that the number of good soldiers capable of fighting in the front rank were limited in his day, making it 'necessary to regulate the depth of the formation according to the type of unit'. The better units could be formed five or seven deep and the worst up to ten deep.

The mounted warrior of the 5th–6th centuries

While infantry remained the decisive arm of the Roman army through the 3rd and 4th centuries, the situation began to change as Roman warlords surrounded themselves with bands of mounted retainers. By the 6th century the *Strategikon* recommends:

'*The general would be well advised to have more cavalry than infantry. The latter is set only for close combat, while the former is easily able to pursue or to retreat, and when dismounted the men are all set to fight on foot.*'

The 6th-century soldier was in fact much more than a cavalryman: he had become an all-round mounted warrior. With his bow he could skirmish at a distance, but he was also heavily armoured and well equipped for close mounted combat. When a steady force was needed to hold ground, he was quite happy to dismount and fight as a heavy infantryman. On many occasions Belisarius took only cavalrymen with him, and when Narses needed steady infantry, he dismounted his cavalry.

With most armies based on cavalry, battles took on a much more fluid appearance than when infantry had formed their backbone. Procopius' battle descriptions are full of fast-moving actions by small groups of mounted men, so much so that they take on an almost 'heroic' flavour, with individual champions challenging one another and performing deeds of daring. The character of these cavalry engagements is brought out by Procopius when he describes a battle against the Persians: 'And both sides kept making advances upon their opponents and retiring quickly, for they were all cavalry.'

While Procopius' battle descriptions seem to emphasise heroic individual deeds, there may be a certain amount of author's licence as he tries to portray his warriors in a Homeric light. The *Strategikon* presents a more disciplined view of 6th-century cavalry, and constantly stresses the importance of maintaining order. For example, it recommends against using trumpets and battle cries:

'*The better silence is observed, the less disturbed will the younger men be and the less excited the horses . . . The battle cry "Nobiscum", which it was customary to shout* when beginning the charge, is in our opinion extremely dangerous and harmful. Shouting it at that moment may cause the ranks to break up. For because of the shout, the more timid soldiers in approaching really close combat may hesitate before the clash, while the bolder, roused to anger, may rashly push forward and break ranks. The same problem occurs with the horses, for they too differ in temperament. The result is that the battle line is uneven and without cohesion; in fact, its ranks may well be broken even before the charge, which is very dangerous.'

Roman cavalrymen of the 5th and 6th centuries employed a mix of skirmish and shock tactics and were effectively equipped for both. When fighting from a distance with bows, their tactics would not have changed much from those described by Zosimus. They would ride up to their opponents in open order and probably in wedge formation to

This gravestone of a cavalryman from an earlier period shows fairly complete scale armour which would also have been worn throughout the later Empire. Gravestones from the 3rd century onwards tended, however, to depict soldiers without their armour; if anything, cavalry armour became more complete in the later Empire. (Colchester and Essex Museum)

facilitate manoeuvre. They would discharge their arrows and, if they made no impression or if faced with a stronger opponent, would wheel away, conforming to the movement by their standard, to withdraw beyond bowshot and then wheel back to face the enemy again. If, on the other hand, their charge and arrow volley caused their opponents to flinch, they would continue to charge forward into close combat.

Shock tactics were used by the *foederati* and other primarily Germanic troops in the Roman army. These soldiers, the ancestors of the medieval knight, did not skirmish at a distance; armed with lances and shields and perhaps supported by Roman or Hun horse archers, they would charge directly at the enemy and attempt to destroy him in close combat. Such a charge is described in the *Strategikon*:

'At the command "Junge" [Close ranks!], *the soldiers close up from the rear for the charge. With the troops marching in close formation, particularly after they have closed in tightly from the flanks, the archers open fire and the command is given: "Percute"* [Charge]. *The dekarchs and pentarchs* [experienced men in the front two ranks] *then lean forward, cover*

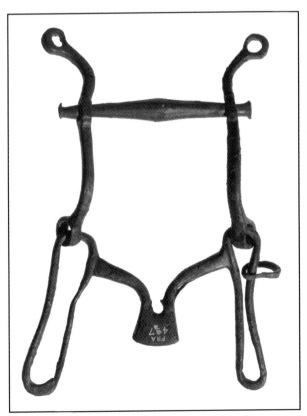

their heads with their shields, hold their lances high as their shoulders in the manner of the fair-haired races, and protected by their shields they ride in good order, not too fast but at a trot, to avoid having the impetus of their charge breaking up their ranks before coming to blows with the enemy, which is a real risk.'*

Cavalry against infantry

Usually cavalry fought cavalry, either on the flanks of the infantry line or, by the 6th century, in all-cavalry battles. They were not expected to charge well-ordered infantry for the simple reason that as long as the infantry held their ground, the cavalry would not be able to force their horses to close. The best cavalrymen could hope to do against steady infantry would be to break their nerve through missile fire combined with the terror of being charged by a mass of horsemen. Against poorly trained foot soldiers with low morale this could succeed. Belisarius' infantry in the Gothic War, for example, usually broke and ran as soon as enemy cavalry approached them. But even second-rate infantry could easily fend off determined cavalry as long as their nerve did not break. At the Battle of Sura in AD 531, for example, Persian cavalry were unable to force their horses to close against a line of unsupported Roman infantry:

'The foot soldiers, and a very few of them, were fighting against the whole Persian cavalry. Nevertheless the enemy were not able either to rout them or in any other way overpower them. For standing shoulder to shoulder they kept themselves massed in a very small space, and they formed with their shields a rigid, unyielding barricade, so that they shot at the Persians more conveniently than they were shot by them. Many a time after giving up, the Persians would advance against them, determined to break up and destroy their line, but they always retired again from the assault unsuccessful. For their horses, annoyed by the clashing of the shields, reared up and made confusion for themselves and their riders.' (Procopius)

On the rare occasions when Roman cavalry faced steady infantry, they would employ typical skirmish tactics: riding up, shooting, wheeling away, then rallying back beyond bow range ready to try again. In

This bit from Newstead is exceptionally severe. The slightest pressure on the reins would drive the spoon into the roof of the horse's mouth, ensuring instant obedience. (National Museums of Scotland)

While mail was perhaps the most common form of protection, scale armour, usually bronze but sometimes iron, was also frequently worn by Roman cavalrymen. Although not quite as flexible as mail, its inflexibility has been over-stressed by some modern writers. Reconstructions have proved that when constructed of small scales, the armour could bend freely with the movement of the body. (National Museums of Scotland)

his description of 2nd-century cavalry games, Arrian describes these tactics against a simulated infantry target:

'Charging in a straight line forwards they then veer to one side, as though turning to make a circle. This turn they make to their right, that is to the spear-throwing side. For thus nothing stands in the way of the javelin throwing, and the shields afford protection to those throwing them as they charge.'

The aftermath of battle

While in theory cavalry could cover the retreat of a defeated army, this rarely seems to have happened. Being more mobile than their infantry counterparts, the cavalry would usually flee the field as soon as things began to go wrong. For example, during the retreat from Persia in AD 363, four legions are named fighting off cataphracts and elephants in a rearguard action with no mention being made of Roman cavalry; and at Adrianople, the Roman cavalry abandoned the infantry to their fate. When the battle had been won, however, the cavalry came to the fore, pursuing and harrying the broken enemy.

Like all soldiers after a successful engagement, the Romans were eager to scour the battlefield for loot. In earlier periods and in infantry-based armies discipline may have been stricter and the men easier to control, but in the multi-racial cavalry armies of the 5th and 6th centuries Roman generals could expect to lose control of their troops once the battle had been won, as Procopius so vividly describes:

'They pursued the fugitives throughout the whole night, killing all the men upon whom they happened, and making slaves of the women and children. . . . Belisarius, seeing the Roman army rushing about in confusion was disturbed [in case the enemy attacked while the men plundered] *. . . for the soldiers, being extremely poor men, upon becoming all of a sudden the masters of great wealth and of women both young and old and extremely comely, were no longer able to restrain themselves . . . For neither did fear of the enemy nor respect for Belisarius occur to them, nor indeed anything at all except the desire for spoils.'*

The author of the *Strategikon* recognised the obvious dangers of such behaviour, and advised that the soldiers should be warned well ahead of time, as is made clear in the military code, that they must absolutely avoid such acts. One suspects, however, that looting was commonplace, particularly in the 6th century, when soldiers were expected to equip themselves from allowances.

One area in which the Roman army stood apart from its opponents is the way in which it was able to provide medical care to its soldiers. Procopius describes some amazing operations after a skirmish during the siege of Rome (see Plate K), and the *Strategikon* advises that 'after the battle the general should give prompt attention to the wounded and see to the burying of the dead. Not only is this a religious duty, but it greatly helps the morale of the living. In fact, the *Strategikon* gives detailed instructions on the use of battlefield medics, recommending that eight to ten men per *bandon*, 'alert, quick, lightly clothed and without weapons' should follow behind their units 'to pick up and give aid to anyone seriously wounded in the battle, or who has fallen off his horse, or is otherwise out of action, so they may not be trampled by the second line or die through neglect of their wounds'.

THE SOLDIER ON CAMPAIGN

We have already seen that during the 3rd and 4th centuries the cavalry played a supporting role in battle and on campaign. (For a full description of a 4th-century campaign see Warrior 9, *Late Roman Infantryman*). This soon changed, and from eyewitness accounts of Procopius we can see that by the 6th century the cavalryman had become an all-round warrior who could be employed in any variety of tasks, from traditional reconnaissance missions to fighting on board ships. Taking Belisarius' campaign against the Vandals (AD 533–34) as an example, we can get a glimpse of what life might have been for a typical soldier engaged on an offensive campaign.

The African campaign (AD 533–34)

The army assembled at Constantinople is recorded as containing 10,000 infantry and 5,000 cavalry, the latter consisting of regular horse archers and lance-armed *foederati*. To this number were added 400 Germanic Eruli, 600 Hunnic Massagetae and an unspecified but large number of Belisarius' personal *bucellarii* (possibly as many as 7,000). The troops embarked on a flotilla of 500 ships. The cargo vessels, carrying men and horses, were escorted by 92 fast fighting ships. It must have been bedlam at the docks as this force, together with thousands of horses and all their provisions, embarked. The loading must have taken days, and everyone would have felt relieved when 'in the seventh year of Justinian's reign [AD 533], at about the spring equinox', they were finally underway.

Difficulties at sea

A sea voyage was no easy undertaking in those days. There were delays due to lack of wind as well as the threat of storms. There was always a danger that in rough winds 'many of the ships should be left behind and scattered on the open seas'. Added to this were the more mundane problems of seasickness and the difficulty of caring for the horses on board. Many animals must have become sick and perhaps died on the voyage. For those soldiers not chronically seasick, boredom would have soon set in, and there were very few things more dangerous than bored soldiers. During a four-day delay for lack of wind, 'two Massagetae killed one of their comrades who was ridiculing them, in the midst of their intemperate drinking, for they were intoxicated'. To lose control of his men this early on would have been disastrous, so Belisarius set a stern example by impaling the culprits, and only narrowly averted a mutiny due to the severity of the punishment.

To make matters worse, disease soon began to take its toll, partly because the bread, which formed the basis of the soldiers' hard rations, had not been properly double-baked to preserve it. Procopius says

This water bottle, similar to those in use in the 18th century, would have been a vital part of the cavalryman's equipment.

It would usually be attached to a saddle horn. (National Museums of Scotland)

that the loaves, which should have stayed hard, disintegrated and turned to a rotten, mouldy flour. 'And the soldiers, feeding upon this . . . became sick and not less than five hundred of them died.' Furthermore, by the time the flotilla reached Sicily, the water of the whole fleet was spoiled.

If at this point the Vandals, who were reasonably good seafarers, had attacked the Roman fleet, the campaign would probably have been over. Not only were the Roman soldiers ill and weary from their journey, but they were 'in mortal dread of sea-fighting. They had no shame in saying beforehand that if they should disembark on land, they would try to show themselves brave men in the battle, but if hostile ships assailed them, they would turn to flight; for, they said, they were not able to contend with two enemies at once, both men and water.' Fortunately for the Romans they were not attacked, since no word of their approach had reached the Vandals; they were able to land on the African coast unopposed.

Infantry are predominant in this siege scene from the Arch of Constantine. During sieges the cavalry would usually be deployed on foraging and scouting duties. The helmets worn by the men on the left are the late Roman style Attic helmets of single bowl construction. They are similar to the classical Attic style, but different enough to make artistic convention unlikely. The men in the town wear ridge-style helmets which, unlike the Attic style, have been confirmed by archeology. (Deutsche Archaologische Institut, Rome)

Establishing a base camp

Procopius recorded a speech by Belisarius which describes the landing procedure:

'We must disembark upon the land with all possible speed, landing horses and arms and whatever else we consider necessary for our use, and we must dig a trench quickly and throw a stockade around us of a kind that can contribute to our safety . . . and with that as our base must carry on the war from there. And if we show ourselves brave men, we shall lack nothing in the way of

provisions, for those who hold the mastery over the enemy are lords also of the enemy's possessions.'

On their first night in an alien land, a long way from home, the soldiers worked hard to set up an almost text-book base camp. Procopius seems to have been amazed that the trench and stockade were completed in one day and that 'the soldiers bivouacked in the camp, setting guards and doing everything else as was customary'. One wonders, however, how impressed Julius Caesar would have been if his legionaries had taken all day to set up camp!

The advance to contact

With a firm base established, the Romans marched out to meet the Vandals. We learn from the *Strategikon* that 'troops moving from their base camp up to combat should take with them spare horses, small tents or a couple of heavy cloaks, the one for covering if needed and the other as a tent or shelter'. They were also instructed to take 20 or 30 lbs of hardtack, flour or other provisions. The soldiers would march out fully equipped, but being still some distance from the enemy, it is quite possible that they would not yet have been wearing their armour. The *Strategikon* recommends leather or wicker cases for carrying coats of mail behind the troopers' saddles so that 'the mail will not be left unprotected and ruined and the soldiers will not be worn out by the constant weight of the armour'.

Belisarius established his order of march with 300 specially picked *bucellarii* in the vanguard. They were to scout far ahead of the main body and report anything they saw of the enemy 'so that they might not be compelled to enter into battle unprepared'. The right flank of the column was protected by the

These troops, from the Arch of Constantine, are in typical undress clothing. On the march the cavalry would screen the front, rear and flanks of the column. (Deutsche Archaologische Institut, Rome)

A close-up view, from the Arch of Constantine, of the typical late Roman pillbox cap worn by soldiers of all ranks and in all branches of the army. (Deutsche Archaologische Institut, Rome)

coast; the Massagetae were detailed to guard the left; and Belisarius himself commanded the rearguard. Their march was unhindered for seven days, and the soldiers would have been in a relaxed mood, helped by the fact that they were able to supplement their hard rations with food purchased at local markets and which the inhabitants were all too happy to furnish (see Plate J). However, Procopius tells us: 'Gelimer [the Vandal king] was following behind without letting it be known to us, except, indeed, on that night when we bivouacked in Grasse, scouts coming from both armies met each other, and after an exchange of blows they each retired to their own camp.'

Preparing for battle

Now battle was imminent and the soldiers would prepare for action. The *Strategikon* recommends that first thing in the morning, when battle is expected, the horses should be watered and each soldier should carry a basic supply of rations in case the operation should become prolonged. True to form, and again recommended by the *Strategikon*, Belisarius gathered the main body of his troops and made a speech of encouragement. 'After speaking these words and uttering a prayer after them, Belisarius left his wife and the barricaded camp to the infantry, and himself

set forth with all the horsemen.' This would not be the last time Belisarius left the infantry behind and fought with cavalry only. Apparently he regarded the infantry as useless, except perhaps for guarding camps. Much later, during the Gothic War, when he was about to do the same thing, some infantry officers pleaded with him to allow them to take part in the battle. Even they had to admit, however, that infantry had done 'little of consequence' in the war, and when they were deployed well to the rear to act as a rallying point for the cavalry, they broke and ran on first contact. Apart from his disregard for the infantry, it is even more illuminating to note that the general was accompanied by his wife. We know that families often accompanied the men on campaign, but although Procopius makes frequent references to Belisarius' wife, he does not mention any other women, so we do not know if the common soldiers did the same thing. Given the great distances and logistical problems, one suspects not.

Unbeknown to the main body, the vanguard of 300 *bucellarii* had already been heavily engaged in combat. It is surprising that they had sent no word back to their commander, particularly as their orders had been to provide advance warning of the enemy and not to become decisively engaged. This is just

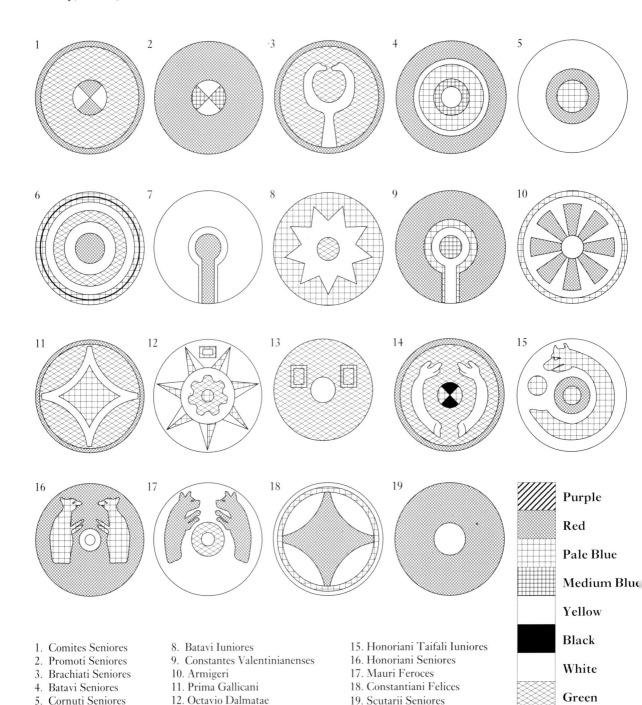

The insignia of the Magister Equitum showing the shield designs of the senior western cavalry units at the end of the 4th century. (Notitia Dignitatum, *Bodleian Library, Oxford*)

1. Comites Seniores
2. Promoti Seniores
3. Brachiati Seniores
4. Batavi Seniores
5. Cornuti Seniores
6. Cornuti Iuniores
7. Alani
8. Batavi Iuniores
9. Constantes Valentinianenses
10. Armigeri
11. Prima Gallicani
12. Octavio Dalmatae
13. Dalmatae Passerentiaei
14. Mauri Alites
15. Honoriani Taifali Iuniores
16. Honoriani Seniores
17. Mauri Feroces
18. Constantiani Felices
19. Scutarii Seniores

Purple
Red
Pale Blue
Medium Blue
Yellow
Black
White
Green

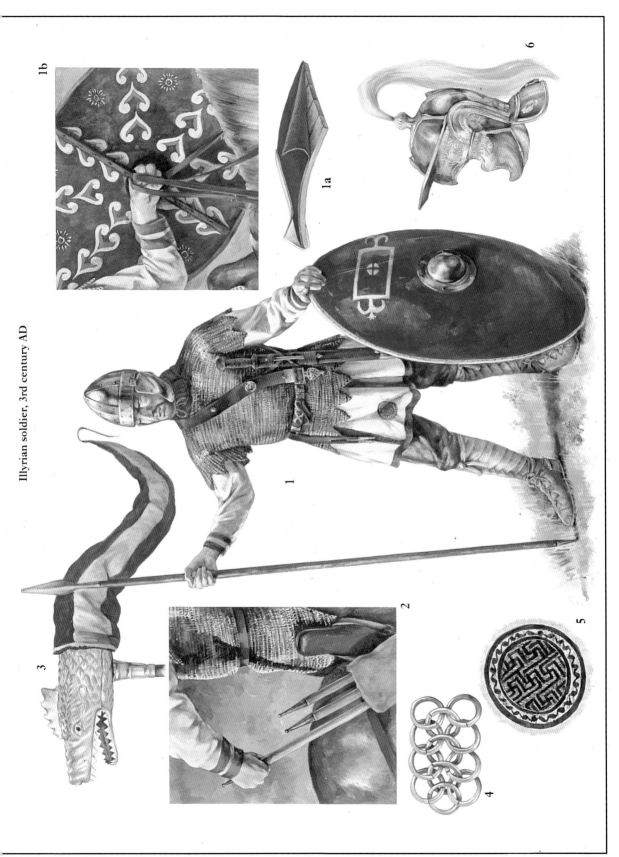

Illyrian soldier, 3rd century AD

A

Cavalry reconnaissance, 3rd century AD

B

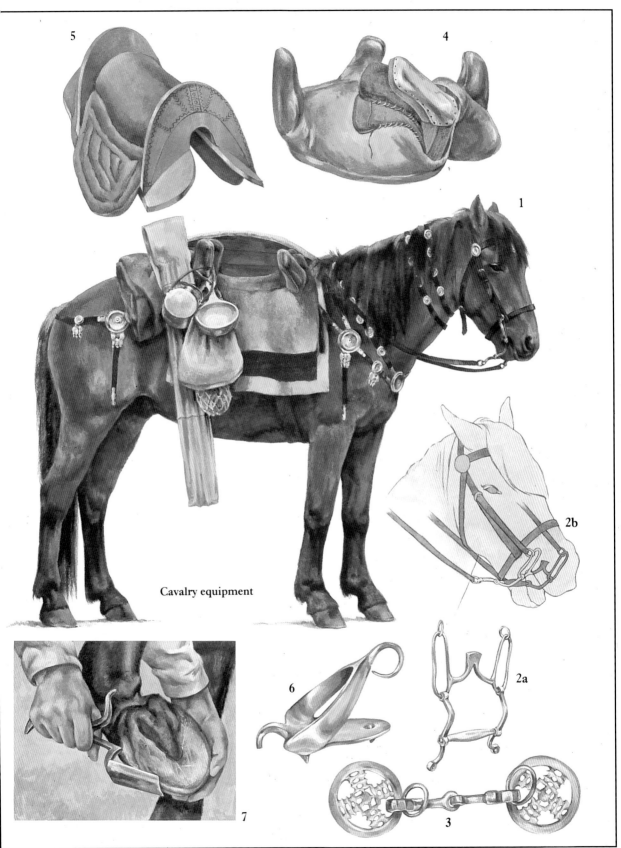

Cavalry equipment

C

Cataphracts in action, Strasbourg, AD 357

D

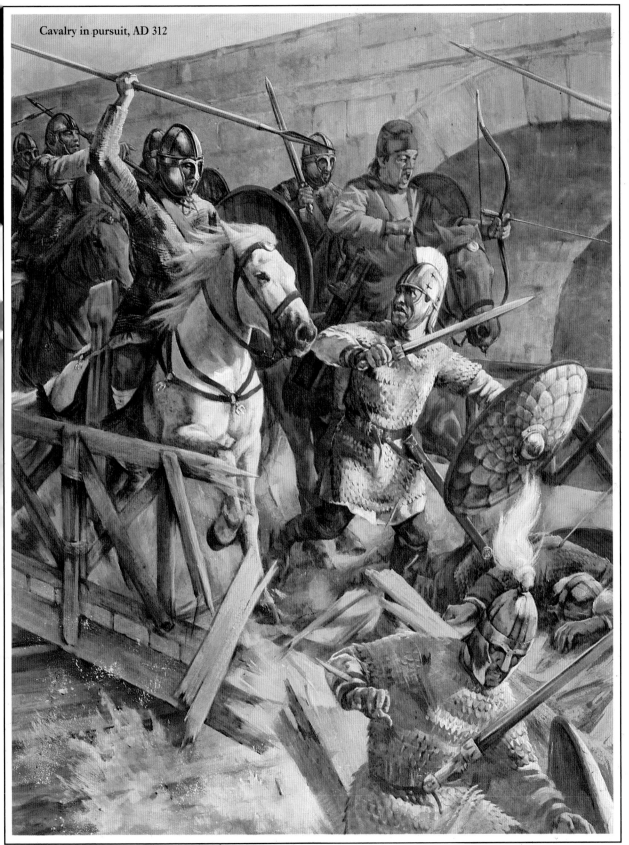

Cavalry in pursuit, AD 312

E

Cavalryman, 4th century AD

F

On parade, Rome AD 357

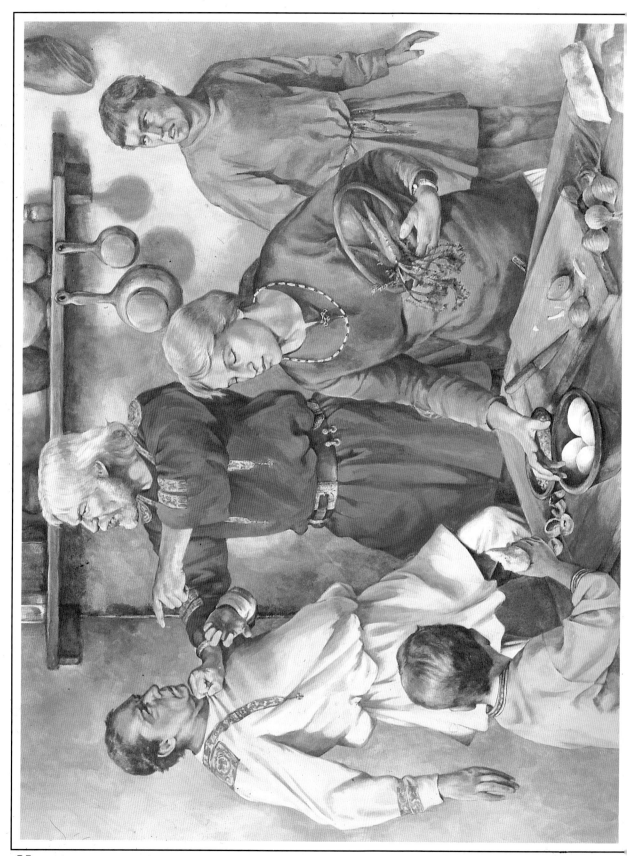

H

Individual training, 5th-6th century AD

J

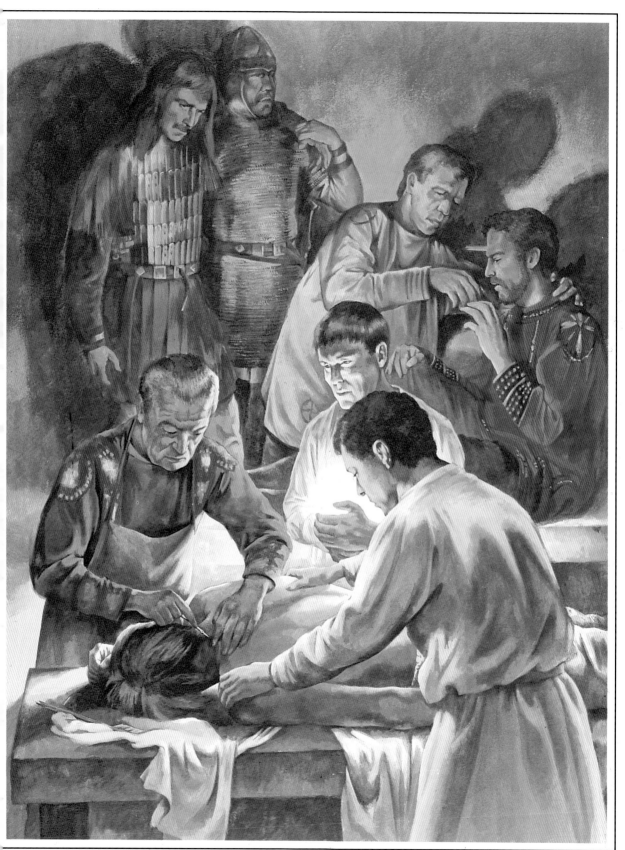

Medical treatment, 6th century AD

K

6th-century horse archer

The Imperial Baths at Trier. Even the towns in the frontier regions had reasonable facilities, making life for the soldiers billeted in the towns fairly comfortable. (Rahmel-Verlag GmbH)

one of many instances where Belisarius' troops, even in elite units, showed a distinct lack of discipline and professionalism. Marching blindly forward, with no idea where the enemy was nor what had happened to their advance guard, the Romans blundered into the Vandals, who were equally lost. The battle developed as a series of fierce skirmishes, with both sides consisting entirely of cavalry. Initially it went well for the Vandals, and they succeeded in routing 800 Roman *bucellarii*. However, they did not press their pursuit vigorously enough, and Belisarius was able to rally the survivors and hit the by now disordered Vandals. The enemy army disintegrated and the way was open to Carthage.

Follow-up actions

With this first major success the tempo of the campaign slowed down. There were other battles, but once the main objective had been captured and later successfully defended, the soldiers of Belisarius' army would have found themselves engaged in the thankless task of pacifying the countryside. The Vandals started to organise a guerilla war, 'by distrib-

uting much money to the farmers among the Libyans. . . . These he commanded to kill Romans who went out into the country, proclaiming a fixed sum of gold for each man killed.. . . And they killed many from the Roman army, not soldiers however, but slaves and servants.'

Procopius describes one incident where Belisarius' aide, Diogenes, went out on a reconnaissance with 22 soldiers. They were seen by Libyan farmers, but since they were too strong for the farmers to kill, the soldiers' presence was reported to Gelimer, who dispatched 300 Vandal cavalry with orders to capture them alive. Diogenes and his men were sleeping on the upper storey of a house when the Vandals reached them at early dawn and sealed off the house. One of the Romans heard the Vandals and quietly roused his companions. Procopius takes up the story:

'Following the opinion of Diogenes, all put on

their clothes quietly and taking up their weapons went below. There they put the bridles on their horses and leaped upon them unperceived by anyone. And after standing for a time in the courtyard entrance, they suddenly opened the door there, and straightway all came out. And the Vandals immediately closed with them, but they accomplished nothing. For the Romans rode hard, covering themselves with their shields and warding off their assailants with their spears. And in this way Diogenes escaped the enemy, losing two of his followers but saving the rest. He himself, however, received three blows in this encounter on the neck and face, from which indeed he came close to dying, and one blow also on his left hand, as a result of which he was thereafter unable to move his little finger.'

Life for the soldiers so far from home, at risk of assassination if they strayed from their units, would have been hard to bear once the initial excitement had worn off. Many deserted and others mutinied, but if they ever wanted to see their homes again they had to continue with their duties, since it would have been impossible to finance a trip home independently. We do not know if troops were rotated after a certain period of time, but one suspects not and probably not many who set out on that spring day in AD 533 ever saw Constantinople again. Some may have remained in Africa, but most probably ended their days in Italy during the terrible Gothic War which was to last another 20 years.

Places to visit

Unfortunately there are very few places to visit that specifically relate to the late Roman period. Most Roman sites and museum collections concentrate on the High Imperial period, which has left more artifacts to posterity. The following suggestions, however, are worth a trip:

Cirencester, Gloucestershire
    Corinium Museum.
Cologne, Germany
    Roemisch-Germanisches Museum.
Dover
    Painted House Museum.
Ephesus, Turkey
    Probably the best preserved Roman ruins of the

The head of a Draco standard. Adopted from the Sarmatians and carried by most late Roman cavalry units, standards played an important part in controlling the movement of cavalrymen. (Staatlisches Amt für Vorund Fruhgeschichte, Koblenz)

period. The city was abandoned in the late Roman period because of plague.

Chesterholm, Cumbria, Hadrian's Wall
> Chesters and Housesteads, Northumberland.

Istanbul, Turkey
> Constantinople, the former eastern capital.

Krefeld, Germany
> Burg Linn museum. Finds from Romano-Merovingian graves.

Leiden, Netherlands
> Rijksmuseum. Magnificent late Roman helmets.

Piercebridge, Durham
> Roman fort from the 4th century.

Ravenna, Italy
> The 5th-century western capital; many mosaics.

Rome
> Arch of Constantine; Aurelian walls; and Vatican Museum.

Saxon Shore Forts
> Burgh Castle, Norfolk; Cardiff Castle, S. Glamorgan; Richborough, Kent; Pevensey, Sussex; Porchester Castle, Hants.

Strasbourg, France
> Musée Archéologique.

Trier, Germany
> One of the 4th-century capitals.

York
> Yorkshire Museum; city walls.

THE PLATES

A: Equites illyricani (3rd century AD)

This man represents one of the Illyrian soldiers, recruited from the frontier regions of the Balkans, who formed the core of the central cavalry reserve of the 3rd century. He is essentially a light cavalryman, and would perform traditional tasks such as patrolling, scouting and screening.

The soldier's main defensive equipment was his shield, which bore a unit design. The shield patterns depicted in the *Notitia Dignitatum* (written more than a century later) show those of the *equites dalmatae* with similar box-like symbols, so this may have been an earlier version. Both round and oval shields were carried. This oval version is based on 3rd-century remains found at Dura Europos. It is about 1.1 m high and 90 cm wide, constructed of

This magnificent gilded silver helmet can be identified as belonging to a soldier of the Equites Stablesiani *in the mid-4th century from an inscription and some coins found with it. (Rijksmuseum van Oudheden, Leiden)*

1 cm thick wood planks, covered and bound with leather (**A1a**). A hollow iron boss, which could also be made of bronze, covers the central hand grip, and the rear of the shield is elaborately painted (**A1b**), probably with an individual pattern rather than an official unit design. Carrying the shield and reins in the same hand would have required considerable skill.

In battle the *equites illyricani* used skirmishing tactics, harassing opponents with javelins then closing in with spear and sword once they were sufficiently weakened. Javelins might have been carried behind the shield, but it was less burdensome to draw them from a case behind the saddle (**A2**). Such cases are depicted on a number of gravestones, and may have originated with steppe peoples such as the Sarmatians, who introduced the windsock *draco* (dragon) standard (**A3**) that was carried by units of *equites illyricani* and later spread throughout the army.

The soldier's light mail shirt provides a fair

A nobleman's country villa. During the 5th century the power of large landowners grew to the point where many employed their own private armies. In addition, poor soldiers in static units sometimes hired themselves out to work the fields of these immense holdings. Both practices were officially illegal but commonplace. (Rheinisches Landesmuseum, Trier)

degree of protection without hindering his mobility. It may not have been issued to him but could have been picked up as battlefield booty or bought. When engaged in relatively safe tasks, the mail shirt could be rolled up and strapped behind the saddle. Roman mail (**A4**) was made with alternating rows of riveted and welded rings.

The soldier is wearing a typical loose-fitting long-sleeved tunic decorated with coloured bands and discs (**A5**). Such patterns were worn throughout the later Empire, by civilians as well as soldiers. This one is based on one of the many surviving samples from Egypt.

Although traditional helmet styles continued (**A6**), the *spangenhelm* style, like the simple version worn by the main figure, was probably typical for the men serving in the Danube frontier regions. It too was adopted from the Sarmatians and became increasingly popular over the next few centuries.

B: Cavalry reconnaissance (3rd century AD)

The cavalry were the eyes and ears of the army. When advancing in enemy territory cavalrymen would scout ahead, looking for signs of the enemy, good routes, potential camp locations, river crossing points, sources of food and water and so on. They would also be used to screen the army from the eyes of enemy scouts. Some might be employed as flank and rear guards or foraging parties. On the defensive cavalry would be used to locate enemy raiders and perhaps impede their progress.

These men, possibly from a detached *vexillation*, are observing the movements of enemy raiders. They are lightly equipped and working in small groups. They rely on cunning and mobility to accomplish their missions, rather than their ability to fight. Consequently, any armour and helmets have been left behind and their equipment is kept to a minimum. Having located the enemy, some men would e detailed to keep an eye on them while others eported back to their parent body, who would then ry to bring up a force strong enough to destroy the aiders. The increased demand for actions such as hese led to a growth in the cavalry arm during the rd century.

Perhaps typically for this anarchic period, the nen show few signs of uniformity. One wears the illbox-style pannonian leather cap which was a universal undress headgear for all ranks from the 3rd o the 5th century. Their clothes and the simple hield design are taken from contemporary mosaics.

C: Cavalry equipment

The Roman cavalryman's horse was smaller than nodern horses: somewhere between 130 cm and 150 m high. Even horses described by ancient writers as large', such as Parthian, Sarmatian and Hunnish reeds, rarely exceeded 155 cm, and would be con-idered of medium size today.

Although the army on the march would be ac-companied by baggage wagons, cavalry would often operate away from the main body. This horse (**C1**) is loaded up for the march with everything the cavalry-man would need to be self-sufficient. His shield, javelin case, waterbottle, cooking utensils and rations are attached to the saddle, and his cloak is rolled up behind. The need to carry such loads, as well as the weight of an armoured rider, for long distances meant that the ideal mount was not a fast, high-spirited horse but rather a horse with high endur-ance.

The cavalryman would be looking for absolute obedience from his mount, since in battle the slight-est mistake could cost him his life. To ensure such

A cavalry charge depicted on the Arch of Constantine. Most cavalry actions consisted of fluid but controlled hit and run tactics. The soldiers would ride up to their opponents hoping to break their *nerve. If this failed, they would wheel sharply away to the right, showering the enemy with missiles, and withdraw to beyond bow range to try again. (Deutsche Archaologische Institut, Rome)*

obedience, some Roman bits, like **C2a** from Newstead, could be extremely severe. The slightest pressure on the reins would drive a plate into the roof of the horse's mouth, causing intense pain (**C2b**). Such bits would not be allowed today, but for a soldier whose life depended on keeping his horse under control in the chaos of a battle while his right hand wielded his weapons and his left held the reins and shield, they were probably very necessary. **C3** is an example of a softer bit, perhaps used by riders better able to control their mounts. Although the Roman cavalryman rode without stirrups, he did

have a well-constructed saddle that allowed him to keep a fairly firm seat even when making energetic upper body movements such as swinging a sword or hurling a javelin. Claims by some writers that cavalry were ineffective prior to the introduction of stirrups have been disproved by modern tests using Roman equipment. **C4** shows how the saddle in use at the start of this period was constructed. It was built around a wooden frame, with the four horns reinforced with bronze plates and then padded and covered with leather. The horns held the rider firmly in the saddle as well as being useful for attaching

These soldiers surrounding the emperor on the Arch of Galerius, although probably infantrymen, show typical 3rd–4th-century full equipment of spangenhelm helmet, full scale armour and large round or oval shields. Note also the typical round disc decoration on the skirt of the emperor's tunic. (Deutsche Archaologische Institut, Rome)

equipment. In the 5th century a new form of wooden frame saddle with quilted padding (**C5**), probably of Hunnic origin, was gradually adopted, and remained in use beyond the end of this period.

Roman horses were rarely shod at the start of this period. Damage to the hooves was avoided by keeping off roads. On the march they would usually go cross-country, screening the front, flanks and rear of the column, and those not engaged in such tasks would probably ride on the side of the road rather than on the hard surface. When necessary, temporary horseshoes like the one at **C6** could be fitted, then removed when no longer required. Conventional horseshoes were rare, at least prior to the 4th century. **C7** shows a hoof-cleaning tool being used.

D: Cataphracts in action (Strasbourg, AD 357)

In one of the few descriptions we have of Roman cataphracts in action, Ammianus Marcellinus describes their defeat at the hands of the Alamannic cavalry (who may have dismounted):

'The Germans rushed forward with more haste than caution, throwing themselves upon our squadrons of horse . . . At the very crisis of battle, when our cavalry were

Although becoming increasingly important, 4th-century cavalry still acted primarily in support of the infantry. (Arch of Constantine, Deutsche Archaologische Institut, Rome)

51

Fanciful weapons like this Currodrepanus Singularis, a scythed chariot driven by a cataphract lancer, were proposed by the anonymous author of a 4th-century treatise as a solution to Rome's military problems. (Bodleian Library, Oxford)

bravely regrouping and the infantry were stoutly protecting their flanks with a wall of serried shields, thick clouds of dust arose and the fight swayed this way and that . . . Our cavalry on the right unexpectedly gave way in disorder. The first to flee, however, blocked the path of those who followed, and when they found themselves safe in the lap of the Legions, they halted and renewed the fight. What caused this incident was that while their ranks were being re-dressed, the Cataphracts saw their commander slightly wounded and one of their comrades slipping over the neck of his horse, which sank under the weight of his armour. They then began to shift each for himself, and would have created total confusion by trampling over the infantry had not the latter, who were being drawn up in very close order, held their ground.'

Typically Ammianus is vague about whether this was a unit of *cataphractarii* or *clibanarii*, and he uses both terms. Since *cataphractarii*, probably of Gallic origin, are more likely in Julian's Gallic army, they have been depicted here as such. Their equipment shows Sarmatian influences: *spangenhelm* helmets, scale armour and the long lance, or *contus*, being wielded in two hands, without a shield. Only a minority of horses are armoured. Perhaps all should have been, but for a second-rate unit in a regional army, full horse armour would have been hard to come by. Many of the horses here only have chamfrons, which the archeological record shows as being fairly common. Although they are often thought to have been used only for cavalry games and

parades, it is highly unlikely that the Romans had any equipment that was solely intended for parade use. Modern tests have shown that horses are frightened by the approach of other horses wearing chamfrons, so they may have had benefits in addition to their protection value.

The *Notitia Dignitatum* lists all *cataphractarii* units except one as being stationed in the east by the 5th century. They may have accompanied Julian from Gaul when he went east in AD 361 and never returned.

E: Cavalry in pursuit (Milvian Bridge, AD 312)

In battle it was not the job of the cavalry to engage infantry. Cavalry would be deployed on the wings of the army to protect the flanks of the infantry and to defeat enemy cavalry. If the opportunity presented itself, they would try to hit the enemy infantry in the flank after their cavalry support had been driven off. Horses could not be made to charge formed bodies of men on foot, but if the infantry lost their formation it was a different story. Then, fighting as individuals, the mounted men would have had a significant advantage. Once an infantryman lost his nerve and broke and ran from his formation, he would be easy meat for a pursuing cavalryman. Describing a battle between Goths and Romans in AD 377, Ammianus Marcellinus says: '. . . the fugitives on either side were pursued by cavalry who hacked at their heads and backs with all their strength.'

This plate, based on a relief from the Arch of Constantine, shows the pursuit and destruction of Maxentius' Praetorians by Constantine's heavy cavalry supported by horse archers. The Praetorians are retreating over a pontoon bridge which has suddenly collapsed in the middle, throwing many of them into the water. All semblance of order has been lost on both sides, and in a clash of disordered individuals the infantry would have had no chance.

The scale pattern depicted for the Praetorians' shields is shown on a 5th-century ivory of Stilicho as well as the 1st-century Cancellaria relief. Presumably it was a traditional guards pattern that remained in use over several centuries.

F: Equites Stablesiani (4th century AD)

This plate depicts a well equipped 4th-century cavalryman. He is probably a long-service veteran who has had the opportunity to kit himself out with some of the best equipment available. Some of it may be booty, some gifts or awards from his superiors, and the remainder purchased. His fine gilded helmet is based on one found at Deurne in the Netherlands, engraved 'STABLESIA VI', so the owner belonged to a unit of *equites stablesiani*. It can be accurately dated to the first quarter of the 4th century from coins of AD 319 found with it.

The cavalryman's side-arm was the *spatha* (**F1a**), a fairly long sword that could be used for stabbing or cutting. This example has a fine pattern-welded blade (**F1b**), made by iron rods twisted together, hammered, cut up and then recombined.

This soldier's closed sandal with spurs (**F2**) is common footwear for cavalrymen of this period.

Typically for northern climates, he wears Germanic-style long trousers with additional wool bindings wrapped around the lower leg. Alternatively he could wear woollen socks like **F3a** which come from Egypt.

The fine tunic, made from a wool-linen mix with wide loose sleeves (**F4**), is based on an example found in Egypt and now in the Trier Staatsmuseum. Such a tunic might have been a private purchase or a gift. Red tunics had had military associations since Hellenistic times and may have been sought out by veteran soldiers to set them apart from the usual undyed civilian tunics. Recruits, however, were probably issued standard undyed or bleached white tunics with a simple uni-colour trim. The elaborate decorative pattern (**F4a**) would no doubt have been quite costly. When the tunic wore out, which would not have taken long on campaign, the decorative trim would have probably been cut off and stitched on to a new tunic.

Alternative helmet styles typical for the period are shown at **F5** and **F6**. The Berkasovo helmet (**F5**) is a simpler version of the Deurne helmet worn by the main figure. It is a 'ridge' helmet, formed by two half bowls held together by a central ridge, with cheek and neck guards added on. The style was typical for the 4th and 5th centuries and probably had Persian origins. The Der-el-Medineh helmet (**F6**), to the *spangenhelm* family. These helmets, of Sarmatian origin, were made up of several plates (usually six; sometimes four) held together by reinforcing bands. This example is similar to those worn by soldiers depicted on the 3rd-century Arch of Galerius, and the style remained popular, with variations, throughout this period and beyond.

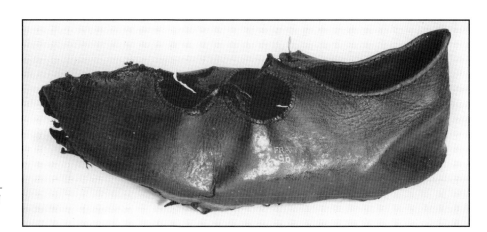

This leather slipper-like shoe is typical of late Roman footwear and is depicted on numerous mosaics from the period – worn both by soldiers and civilians. (National Museums of Scotland)

G: Parades and processions (Clibanarii, Rome, AD 357)

'The emperor's person was surrounded by purple banners woven in the form of dragons and attached to the tops of gilded and jewelled spears . . . On each side marched a file of men-at-arms with shields and plumed helmets, whose shining breastplates cast a dazzling light. At intervals were cataphracts, the so-called clibanarii, *wearing masks and equipped with cuirasses and belts of steel . . . Their limbs were entirely covered by a garment of thin circular plates fitted to the curves of the body and so cunningly articulated that it adapted itself to any movement the wearer needed to make.'*

The unit of armoured cavalry depicted here is the *Scola Scutariorum Clibanariorum*, one of the new guards units created by Constantine to replace the Praetorians, who were disbanded after Milvian Bridge. Constantius (337–61) is credited with introducing Persian-style cataphracts (called *clibanarii*) into the Roman army.

Given the occasion and the status of the unit, the soldiers' equipment, which shows Persian origin, is far more uniform and elaborate than one might find in a line unit on campaign. The Romans understood the psychological importance of impressive military displays. The *Strategikon*, for example, notes that 'the more handsome the soldier is in his armament, the more confidence he gains in himself and the more fear he inspires in the enemy'.

The body armour worn by the *clibanarii* is modelled on the graffiti of a 3rd-century Persian *clibanarius* from Dura Europos, and the horse armour from examples found there. Both bronze and iron scales were used. A variety of helmets are shown. They are all of the ridge style with additional face, cheek and neck protection. The helmet worn by the left hand figure is a reconstruction of a Persian helmet found at Dura Europos.

H: Billeting the field army (Italy, 5th century AD)

Units of the mobile field armies did not have permanent quarters. When on campaign they would live under canvas, and at other times they were billeted on the local population. The ordinary citizen had to surrender one-third of his house to a soldier, which often resulted in friction between 'host' and 'guest'. Hosts were not required to provide anything other than bare rooms, but we have many examples of soldiers extorting food, bedding and oil, and even ordering baths. These demands for extra services were known as *Salgamum*, and a series of laws in the

The Roman saddle through to the end of the 4th century was characterised by four horns reinforced with these bronze plates. The horns ensured the rider kept a firm seat, and were useful for attaching equipment. (National Museums of Scotland)

4th–6th centuries officially forbade it. A ruling in 340 states that 'hosts' could voluntarily provide such things. Presumably it would have been fairly easy for a soldier to create the circumstances by which a householder might be persuaded to 'volunteer' more than he had to. An account from Edessa between 503 and 505 tells of soldiers turning people out of their homes, beating them up, stealing clothes and belongings and exacting oil, wood and salt. An official complaint to the local commander resulted in a ruling that the soldiers were entitled to a bed, bedding, firewood and oil – in contravention of the imperial laws prohibiting *Salgamum*.

Soldiers had been allowed to marry since the reign of Septimus Severus, and were accompanied by their families, sometimes even on campaign. In this scene a German soldier of the Italian field army, together with his family, are extorting food from their Italian host. The normal friction between host and guest must have been greatly increased by the fact that the vast majority of the soldiers, particularly in the west, were Germans with different language, customs and possibly religion. Great difficulties arose, for example, when Julian's primarily pagan Celtic and Germanic troops were stationed in Greek-speaking Christian Antioch.

I: Individual training (5th–6th century AD)

While horse archers had always been present in the Roman army, they had been a small minority and were typically lightly equipped skirmishers. During the 5th century, under the influence of the Persians and Huns, the cavalry began to adopt the bow as their primary weapon, so that by the time of Belisarius'

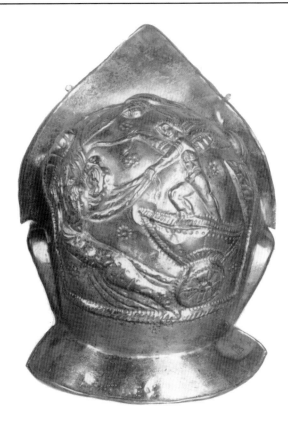

Closed helmets like this example are described by Arrian for use in cavalry sports. Restricted vision would have made them less useful in combat, but since some descriptions of cataphracts mention face-masks it is possible that they were used in action. (National Museums of Scotland)

campaigns of the 6th century the typical Roman cavalryman had become a horse archer. Unlike earlier horse archers, these soldiers were quite heavily armoured and were capable of fighting hand-to-hand as well as skirmishing. Some of them, probably the better trained *bucellarii*, could be armed with spears as well as swords and bows. Individual training for such all-round warriors would have been quite intensive. The *Strategikon* gives us an idea of what the individual cavalryman was expected to do:

'On horseback at a run he should fire one or two arrows rapidly and put the strung bow in its case, then he should grab the spear which he has been carrying on his back. With the strung bow in its case, he should hold the spear in his hand, then quickly replace it on his back and grab the bow.'

Such exercises would have required expert horsemanship as well as proficient weapons handling, and could have been expected only of the better units. Lesser trained soldiers probably specialised either as horse archers or spearmen; German *foederati* would have provided most of the spearmen. We do not know how dual-armed soldiers attached their spears to their backs; there was probably a loop around the middle of the shaft that could be hooked over an attachment to a baldric.

J: Camp life (Grasse, N. Africa, AD 533)

The rigid camp discipline of the earlier Roman army had long been replaced by a more flexible and relaxed approach. In hostile country, camps might still be fortified, but this was not necessarily routine. The *Strategikon* recommends that fortifications be constructed 'even though the army might stay there only for a day', but it is doubtful that this advice was always followed. Temporary fortifications might be little more than a wagon laager or a scattering of caltrops around the perimeter. Procopius' contemporary descriptions of camps during Belisarius' North African campaign paint a rather relaxed picture:

'We made camp as thoroughly secure as the circumstances permitted . . . The inhabitants furnished a mar-

This 5th-century wood carving from Egypt depicts Roman garrison troops defending a town against raiders. Only on rare occasions did such static troops have to engage in combat. Most actions were now fought by the bands of mounted warriors who formed the field armies. (Museuum für Spätantike und Byzantinische Kunst, Berlin)

Making use of tools such as these, armourers, who were attached to most Roman units, could repair damaged equipment as well as re-using battlefield salvage to forge new weapons. (National Museums of Scotland)

ket and served the soldiers in whatever they wished . . . In that place was a palace of a ruler of the Vandals and a park the most beautiful of all we know. For it is excellently watered by springs and has a great wealth of woods. And all the trees are full of fruit; so that each one of the soldiers pitched his tent among fruit trees, and all of them ate their fill of the fruit which was then ripe.'

It is interesting to note that the soldiers on this campaign apparently had allowances from which they were expected to purchase food and supplies from local sources. Some supplies must have been carried: the '20 or 30 lbs of hard tack, flour or some other provisions', suggested by the *Strategikon*, for example. If this is what constituted a campaign ration, soldiers would have been eager to supplement it from local market and very pleased to find such a free supply of fresh fruit.

K: Medical treatment (6th century AD)

Each unit had its own *medicus* (doctor), and medical treatment was of a higher standard than at any other time in Western history until the modern era. This scene is based on descriptions by Procopius of the treatment of three men wounded in a skirmish during the siege of Rome.

The central figure, Arzes, was one of Belisarius' Guards, who had been hit by an arrow between the nose and the right eye. *'The point of the arrow penetrated as far as the neck behind, but it did not show*

through, but the rest of the shaft projected from his face. . . . The physicians wished to draw the weapon from his face but were reluctant to do so, not so much on account of the eye, which they supposed could not be saved, but for fear lest, by cutting the membranes and tissues such as are very numerous in that region, they should cause the death of a man who was one of the best of the household

These triangular Roman arrowheads attached to reconstructed shafts would have been able to pierce armour at short range. (National Museums of Scotland)

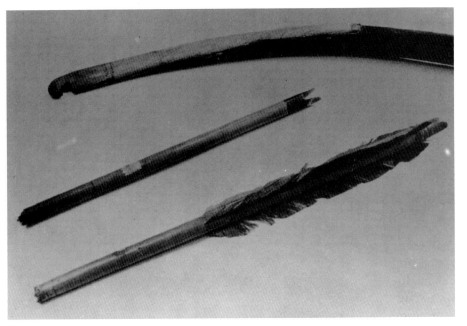

During the 5th century, under the influence of the Huns and Persians, archery became increasingly important, so that by the 6th century the typical Roman cavalryman had become an armoured horse archer. Roman bows were of composite construction; the arrows often of cane or reed with the feathers glued on. (Dura Europos)

of Belisarius. But one of the physicians, Theoctistus by name, pressed on the back of his neck and asked whether he felt much pain. And when the man said that he did, he inferred that the barb of the weapon had penetrated to a point not far from the skin. Accordingly he cut off that part of the shaft which showed outside and threw it away, and cutting open the skin at the back of the head, at the place where the man felt most pain, he easily drew toward him the barb, which with its three sharp points now stuck out behind and brought with it the remaining portion of the weapon. Thus Arzes remained entirely free from serious harm and not even a trace of the wound was left on his face.'

In the background is Cutilas, a Thracian officer who had a javelin embedded in the middle of his head, and when the javelin was drawn rather violently from his head (for it was very deeply embedded) 'he fell into a swoon' (and later died).

The soldier being helped into the hospital room is Bochas, whom Procopius describes as a 'youthful' Hun who had been wounded by one spear thrust 'where his armour did not cover him, above the right armpit, very close to the shoulder' and another spear thrust which had 'struck him in front and pierced his left thigh, and cut the muscles there'. (He died three days later.)

L: 6th-century horse archer

Armoured horse archers formed the bulk of the 6th-century armies. His equipment – bow and sword but no spear, plumed 'attic'-style helmet, scale armour with *pteruges* (leather strips) covering the shoulders and thighs, no shield – is from a contemporary Egyptian ivory and is probably representative of garrison troops of the period. This helmet type is very common in art from the 4th century on, but has not been confirmed by archeological finds. It is quite possible that armouries in Greek parts of the Empire continued to produce helmets that followed Hellenistic styles, with single bowl construction rather than the more common multi-part *spangenhelm* or 'ridge' styles. Scale armour had a long tradition in the east, and was a fairly inexpensive form of defence. It was less flexible than mail, however, requiring the addition of *pteruges* to provide some protection to the vulnerable thighs and shoulders. Injuries such as those sustained by Bochas (see Plate K) were presumably quite common with this form of armour.

Roman medical instruments. The well developed system of medical care was unrivalled in Europe until the modern era. (National Museums of Scotland)

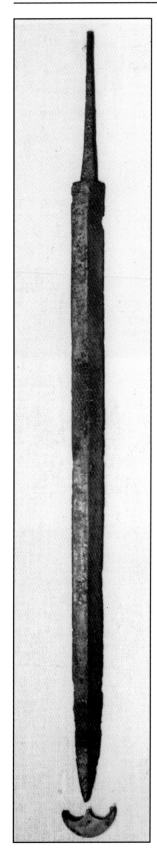

The cavalryman's main side-arm was the fairly long spatha, worn on the left side suspended either from a baldric or from the waist-belt. This is a surviving blade together with a scabbard chape. (National Museums of Scotland)

This 6th-century Egyptian ivory depicts a cavalryman equipped according to the description by Procopius. He wears scale armour with pteruges, a late Roman Attic-style helmet and carries a bow but no spear or shield. Although

Procopius says that some cavalrymen carried spears as well as bows, probably only elite units like the Bucellarii reached a sufficiently high level of training to handle both weapons. (Rheinisches Landesmuseum, Trier)

The dismounted figure represents the same man after some hard but financially successful campaigning against the Goths in Italy. He carries much of his wealth on his person, in the form of Gothic jewellery looted from the battlefield, a fine Italian-made *spangenhelm* and new tunic and trousers. The wide trousers were popular with 6th-century soldiers and probably originated on the steppes. They would have been more comfortable than tight wool hose when campaigning in hot climates. The soldier's cloak and armour are a bit the worse for wear, and no doubt he would have been looking to replace them as soon as possible. He still fights as a horse archer, but, having being called on to fight in close combat on several occasions, he has added a small shield to his defensive equipment.

GLOSSARY

Alamanni A confederation of German tribes who were one of Rome's main opponents in this period. Their descendants are the modern Alsatians, Swiss Germans and inhabitants of most of Baden.

Auxilia A new type of unit created at the end of the 3rd century with a full strength of about 500 men.

Bandon A 6th-century unit of about 300 cavalrymen.

Bucellarii Personal retainers of magnates and warlords.

Bucellatum Dried biscuit or hard tack which formed part of the soldier's field rations.

Cataphract A heavily armoured cavalryman modelled either on the Sarmatians (*cataphractarius*) or the Persians (*clibanarius*). His horse might also have been armoured.

Comitatenses Line troops of the mobile field army.

Comites An honorific title given to some senior cavalry units.

Dekarch Commander of ten men and file leader in 6th-century cavalry units.

Draco A windsock-style dragon standard, adopted from the Sarmatians and carried by most cavalry units.

Eques An ordinary cavalry trooper.

Equites The cavalry.

Fabricae State-run arms factories.

Foederati (federates) Foreign troops serving in the Roman army under their own leaders.

Hasta A spear.

Illyria A Roman province roughly equating to the former Yugoslavia. It was a major source of recruits, particularly in the 3rd century.

Illyriciani (Equites illyriciani) Troops of the central cavalry reserve formed in the 3rd century, and consisting of *promoti* (former legionary cavalry), *dalmatae* (recruited from Illyria), *mauri* (from North Africa) and *scutarii* (probably heavier cavalry).

Isuaria A mountainous area of Asia minor and source of many 6th-century infantry recruits.

Lancea A light spear that could either be thrown or retained for hand-to-hand combat; probably the preferred weapon of the later Roman infantryman.

Limes Frontier zones.

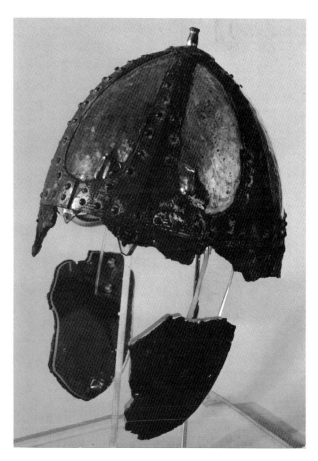

This spangenhelm *from Alsace is typical of the style worn in the 6th century by Romans and Germans. It differs from earlier examples by having a smaller nose guard and no neck guard. Many, however, would have had an attached mail aventail to protect the back of the head. (Musee Archeologique, Strasbourg)*

Limitanei Static border troops.

Lorica Armour. Types used in this period include: *segmentata* (segmented plate armour); *hamata* (mail); *squamata* (scale); and *lamellar* (small vertical iron plates).

Notitia Dignitatum A list of offices of the late Roman administration, for the latter part of the 4th and the early 5th centuries. It includes a fairly complete listing of army units and shield designs.

Palatini Elite troops of the mobile field army.

Pentarch Leader of five men, forming the second rank in 6th-century cavalry units.

Phalerae Metal discs decorating the horse harness.

Psuedocomitatenses *Limitanei* transferred to the field army.

Pteruges Leather strips covering the shoulders and thighs. Part of an undergarment worn under armour.

Sagittarii Archers.

Salgamum The practice of soldiers demanding more of their hosts than was required when soldiers were billeted on the local population.

Scholae The all-cavalry imperial guards formed by Constantine to replace the Praetorians.

Spangenhelm A conical segmented helmet of Danubian origin worn throughout this period.

Spatha A fairly long sword that was the favoured side-arm of the period.

Strategikon A military manual written at the end of the 6th century.

Vegetius Flavius Vegetius Renatus. A 5th-century writer who produced a military treatise lamenting the demise of the classical heavy legions and urging improvements in training and equipment.

Vexillatio In the 3rd century, a detachment of a larger unit; later a cavalry unit of about 500–600 men.

BIBLIOGRAPHY

Primary sources
Arrian, *Against the Alans: The Tactica*.
Procopius of Caesarea, *History of the Wars*.
Ammianus Marcellinus, *The Histories*.
Mauricius, *The Strategikon*.
The Notitia Dignitatum.
Flavius Vegetius Renatus, *The Art of War*.
Zosimus, *The New History*.

Secondary sources
Barker, P., *The Armies & Enemies of Imperial Rome* (Worthing, 1981)
Bachrach, B.S., *A History of the Alans in the West* (Minneapolis, 1973)
Bishop, M.C. and Coulston, J.C.N., *Roman Military Equipment* (London, 1993)
Bona, I., *The Dawn of the Dark Ages* (Budapest, 1976)
Boss, R., *Justinian's Armies* (Stockport, 1993)
Burns, T., *A History of the Ostrogoths* (Bloomington, Indiana, 1984)
Bury, J.B., *History of The Later Roman Empire* (New York, 1958)
Connolly, P., *The Roman Cavalryman* (Oxford, 1988)
Coulston, J.C.N., *Late Roman Armour, 3rd–6th Centuries AD, Journal of Roman Military Equipment Studies* I (London, 1990)
Christodoulou, D., *Byzantine Complexities II, Unit Organisation and Nomenclature (AD 500–600), Slingshot*, Vol 147
Delbrueck, H., *Geschichte der Kriegskunst im Rahmen der Politischen Geschichte* (Berlin, 1921)
Dixon, K. and Southern, P., *The Roman Cavalry* (London, 1992)
Dodgeon, M. and Lieu, S., *The Roman Eastern Frontier and the Persian Wars AD 226–363* (London, 1991)
Dupuy & Dupuy, *The Encyclopaedia of Military History* (New York, 1970)
Ferrill, A., *The Fall of the Roman Empire – the Military Explanation* (London, 1986)
Fuentes, N., *The Roman Military Tunic, Proceedings of the 3rd Roman Military Equipment Conference* (1987)
Gibbon, E., *The Decline and Fall of the Roman Empire* (New York, Modern Library, no date)
Gordon, C.D., *The Age of Attila* (Toronto, 1966)
Hoffman, D., *Das Spaetroemische Bewegungsheer und die Notitia Dignitatum* (Duesseldorf, 1970)
Hyland, A., *Equus, The Horse in the Roman World* (London, 1990)
Hyland, A., *Training the Roman Cavalry* (London, 1993)
James, S., *Evidence from Dura Europos for the Origins of Late Roman Helmets, Revue d'Art Oriental et d'Archéologie* (Paris, 1986)
Jones, A.H.M., *The Later Roman Empire* (Oklahoma University Press, 1964)

Johnson, S., *Later Roman Britain* (Norfolk, 1980)

Junkelmann, M., *Die Reiter Roms*, 3 vols (Mainz, 1992)

Keegan, J., *The Face of Battle* (London, 1976)

Lot, F., *The End of the Ancient World and the Beginnings of the Middle Ages* (Trans. New York, 1961)

Luttwak, E.N., *The Grand Strategy of the Roman Empire* (London, 1976)

Maenchen-Helfen, O.J., *The World of the Huns* (Los Angeles, 1973)

MacDowall, S., *Late Roman Infantryman* (London, 1994)

Moss, J.R., *The Effects of the Policies of Aetius on the History of Western Europe, Historia LXXII* (1973)

Nauerth, C., *Die Koptischen Textilien der Sammlung Wilhelm Rautenstrauch im Staedtischen Museum Simeonstift Trier* (Trier, 1989)

Ardant du Picq, *Battle Studies* (Trans. Harrisburg, 1947)

Robinson, H.R., *What the Soldiers Wore on Hadrian's Wall* (Newcastle-upon-Tyne, 1976)

Robinson, H.R., *The Armour of Imperial Rome* (London, 1975)

Taeckholm, U., *Aetius and the Battle on the Catalaunian Fields, Opuscula Romana VII* (1969)

Theocharadis, P.L., *Late Roman and Early Byzantine Helmets, Proceedings of the 1st International Symposium on Everyday Life in Byzantium* (Athens, 1989)

Randers-Pehrson, J.D., *Barbarians & Romans* (Kent, 1983)

Wallace-Hadrill, J.M., *The Barbarian West* (New York, 1961)

Notes sur les planches en couleur

A Equites illyriconi (3ème siècle ap. J.C.) **A1(a)** Ombon de fer creux **(b)** Motif de l'envers du bouclier; **A2** étui contenant des javelots; **A3** étendard *draco* (dragon) de Windstock; **A4** Cotte de mailles romaine comportant des rangs alternés de mailles rivetées et soudées; **A5** Tunique typique lâche à manches longues avec bandes et disques colorés; **A6** Casque *spangelhelm* typique du style porté par les troupes stationnées sur la frontière du Danube.

B Reconnaissance de cavalerie (3ème siècle ap. J.C.) La cavalerie représentait les yeux et les oreilles de l'armée principale, surtout en territoire ennemi. Ces hommes observent les mouvements des maraudeurs ennemis en s'appuyant sur leur rapidité et leur mobilité plutôt que sur leur capacité de combat. D'où leur manque d'armures et de matériel.

C Matériel de cavalerie **C1** Le cheval porte tout ce dont le soldat de cavalerie peut avoir besoin en campagne; **C2(a)** positionnement du mors et des reines **(b)** mors rudimentaire pour le contrôle immédiat du cheval; **C3** mors plus souple; **C4** construction d'une selle du début de cette période; **C5** modèle plus récent, de la période Hunnique; **C6** Fer à cheval temporaire; **C7** outil pour nettoyer les sabots.

D Cataphractes en action (Strasbourg AD 357) Vaincus par la cavalerie Alémanique démontée. Ils portent du matériel influencé par les Samaritains: casques *spangelhelm*, armure à écailles et la longue lance, ou *cotus*, qui était soudée dans les deux mains. Ils se peut qu'ils aient accompagné Julian depuis la Gaule lorsqu'il se déplaça vers l'est en 361 av. J.C. pour ne jamais revenir.

E Cavalerie en cours de poursuite (Milvan Bridge, 312 av. J.C.) Cette planche s'inspire d'un bas-relief de l'Arc de Constantine et illustre la poursuite et la destruction des Prétoriens de Maxebtius par la cavalerie lourde de Constantine, soutenue par des archers à cheval. Une infanterie en formation bien disciplinée pouvait facilement se mesurer à la cavalerie mais comme on le voit ici, en désordre les soldats d'infanterie étaient des cibles faciles.

F Equites Stablesiani (4ème siècle av. J.C.) Un soldat de cavalerie du 4ème siècle bien équipé, sans doute un vétéran étant donné son matériel de grande qualité. **F1(a)** *spatha*, long glaive; **(b)** lame soudée fabriquée à partir de tiges de fer; **F2** sandale fermée avec éperons, chaussures communément portées par les soldats de cavalerie; **F3(a)** Chaussettes de laine égyptiens; **F4** Tunique en laine et lin basée sur un exemple retrouvé en Egypte **F4(a)** Motif décoratif cousu; **F5** Casque berk*asovo*; **F6** Casque *der-el-Medineh*.

G Parades et processions (Rome 357 av. J.C.) Unité de cavalerie avec armures, *scola scutariorum clibanariorum*. Ces unités furent créés par Constantine pour remplacer la Garde Prétorienne qui fut dispersée après Milvan Bridge. Avec leur uniforme de style perse, ils devaient créer une impression de supériorité immédiate.

H cantonnement de l'armée en campagne (Italie, 5ème siècle) Les armées en campagne n'avaient pas de quartiers permanents et, durant les campagnes, pouvaient vivre soit sous tente soit être cantonnées auprès de membres de la population locale qui devaient abandonner un tiers de leur maison à un soldat, pratique qui provoquait souvent des 'frictions'.

I Entraînement individuel (5ème-6ème siècle ap. J.C.) Archer à cheval protégé par

Farbtafeln

A Equites illyricani (3. Jahrhundert n.Chr.) **A1(a)** Hohler Schildbuckel aus Eisen; **(b)** Inneres Schildmuster; **A2** Hülle mit Speeren; **A3** *Draco* (Drachen) Standarte mit Windsack; **A4** Römischer Kettenpanzer, der aus abwechselnden Reihen genieteter und geschweißter Ringe besteht; **A5** Typische, lose Tunika, die mit bunten Bändern und Scheiben verziert ist; **A6** Spangenhelm, typisch für die Art von Helm, die beim Frontdienst an der Donau getragen wurde.

B Kavallerie-Spähtrupp (3. Jahrhundert v.Chr.) Die Kavallerie war sozusagen das Auge und Ohr der Hauptarmee, insbesondere auf feindlichem Gebiet. Diese Männer beobachten die Bewegung des Feindes, wobei sie sich auf Deckung und ihre Beweglichkeit verlassen und auf ihre Kampfkraft, daher tragen sie keine Rüstung und haben keine Ausrüstung bei sich.

C Kavallerie-Ausrüstung **C1** Das Pferd trägt alles, was der Kavallerist auf dem Feldzug braucht; **C2(a)** Anordnung des Gebisses und der Zügel, **(b)** Hartes Gebiß zur sofortigen Beherrschung des Pferdes; **C3** Weicheres Gebiß; **C4** Aufbau des Sattels aus der früheren Periode; **C5** Späteres Modell aus der Hunnenzeit; **C6** Provisorisch angebrachtes Hufeisen; **C7** Werkzeug zum Auskratzen der Hufe.

D Gepanzerte Männer beim Einsatz (Straßburg 357 n.Chr.) Von der abgesessenen alemannischen Kavallerie besiegt. Die Männer tragen eine Ausrüstung, die samaritanische Einflüsse zeigt: den Spangenhelm, Schuppenpanzer und die lange Lanze, oder *cotus*, die mit beiden Händen gefaßt wurde. Unter Umständen begleiteten sie Julius aus Gallien, als er 361 n.Chr. nach Osten zog und nie zurückkehrte.

E Kavallerie bei der Verfolgung (Milvische Brücke, 312 n.Chr.) Diese Farbtafel beruht auf einem Relief vom Konstantinbogen und zeigt die Verfolgung und den Sieg über die Prätorianer des Maxentius durch die schwere Kavallerie von Konstantin, die von Bogenschützen zu Pferde unterstützt wurde. Gut disziplinierte Infanterie in Formation konnte sich durchaus gegen die Kavallerie behaupten, wenn sie jedoch wie hier zersplittert war, so stellte sie ein leichtes Ziel dar.

F Equites Stableslani (4. Jahrhundert n.Chr.) Gut ausgerüsteter Kavallerist aus dem 4. Jahrhundert, wahrscheinlich dienstälterer Veteran, was aufgrund seiner qualitativ guten Ausrüstung zu vermuten ist. **F1(a)** Spatha, bzw. Langschwert; **(b)** geschweißte Klinge aus Eisenstangen; **F2** Geschlossene Sandale mit Sporen, gängiges Schuhwerk unter den Kavalleristen; **F3(a)** Ägyptische Wollsocken; **F4** Tunika aus Wollstoff und Leinen, die auf einem in Ägypten gefundenen Exemplar beruht; **F4(a)** Aufgestickte Verzierung; **F5** *Berkasovo*-Helm; **F6** *Der-el-Medineh*-Helm.

G Paraden und Umzüge (Rom, 357 n.Chr.) *Scola Scutariorum Clibanariorum*, Kavallerie-Einheit in Rüstung. Diese Einheit wurde von Konstantin geschaffen und sollte die Prätorianer, die kaiserliche Leibwache, nach deren Auflösung im Anschluß an die Niederlage an der Milvischen Brücke ersetzen. Der Stil der Kleidung ist persisch, und die Einheit sollte unmittelbar den Eindruck der Überlegenheit schaffen.

H Einquartierung der Feldtruppen (Italien, 5. Jahrhundert) Die Feldtruppen hatten kein ständiges Quartier und mußten daher bei Feldzügen entweder in Zelten campieren oder sie wurden bei Einheimischen einquartiert, die ein Drittel ihrer

une lourde armure, influencé par la cavalerie hun et perse au niveau du style et des armes. Ces archers maniaient leur arc à la perfection mais ils devaient aussi se battre au corps à corps si nécessaire. Leur entraînement était donc intensif et très physique.

J La vie de camp (Grasse, Afrique du Nord 533 av. J.C.) La discipline était très souple, à la différence des premières armées romaines, mais le camps était fortifié s'il se trouvait en territoire ennemi. Ces fortifications se limitaient cependant à un rempart de chars à boeufs ou à quelques chausse-trapes éparpillées sur le pourtour.

K Traitement médical. Chaque unité possédait son propre *medicus* (médecin) et les traitements étaient les meilleurs de toute l'histoire occidentale jusqu'à nos jours. Cette planche représente trois soldats : Arzes, l'un des gardes de Belisarius, Cutilas, un officier de Thrace et Bochas, un jeune Hun. Ils ont tous reçu de graves blessures durant le combat.

L Archer à cheval au 6ème siècle Les chevaux caparaçonnés représentaient la plus grande partie des armées du 6ème siècle. Son matériel, un arc et un glaive mais pas de lance, son casque à panache de style 'attique', son armure à écailles avec *pteruges* (bandes de cuir) qui recouvrent les épaules et les cuisses, pas de bouclier, provient d'une sculpture égyptienne contemporaine sur ivoire et représente sans doute les troupes en garnison à l'époque. La figure debout représente le même homme après une campagne difficile mais financièrement lucrative contre les Goths en Italie.

Behausung einem Soldaten zur Verfügung stellen mußten, was oft zu "Spannungen" führte.

I Einzelausbildung (5.-6. Jahrhundert n.Chr.) Bogenschütze zu Pferde in schwerer Rüstung. Der Stil und die Waffen zeigen Einflüsse der Kavallerie der Hunnen und der Perser. Die Männer konnten ausgezeichnet mit dem Bogen umgehen, wurden jedoch im Bedarfsfall auch im Kampf von Mann zu Mann eingesetzt, daher war die Ausbildung intensiv und körperlich sehr anstrengend.

J Das Leben im Lager (Grasse, Nordafrika, 533 n.Chr.) Im Gegensatz zu den frührömischen Soldaten herrschte hier eine flexible Disziplin. Auf feindlichem Gebiet wurde das Lager jedoch befestigt, obwohl es sich dabei meistens nur um eine Wagenburg oder einige Fußangeln um das Lager herum handelte.

K Ärztliche Betreuung Jede Einheit verfügte über ihren eigenen *Medicus* (Arzt), und die medizinische Betreuung war bis zur modernen Ära besser als zu anderen Zeiten in der westlichen Geschichte. Diese Tafel zeigt drei Soldaten: Arzes, eine der Wachen von Belisarius; Cutilas, einen thrazischen Offizier und Bochas, einen jungen Hunnen. Alle drei wurden beim Gefecht schwer verletzt.

L Bogenschütze zu Pferde aus dem 6. Jahrhundert Gepanzerte Pferde stellten den Hauptteil der Armee im 6. Jahrhundert dar. Die Ausrüstung des Schützen besteht aus Bogen und Schwert, der Speer fehlt. Er trägt einen Helm mit Federbusch im "attischen" Stil, Schuppenpanzer mit "pteruges" (Lederstreifen), die die Schultern und Schenkel bedecken. Er hat keinen Schild. Die Abbildung beruht auf einer zeitgenössischen ägyptischen Elfenbeinschnitzerei und ist wahrscheinlich für die Garnisonstruppen dieser Zeit repräsentativ. Die abgesessene Figur zeigt den gleichen Mann nach einem schwierigen, jedoch finanziell erfolgreichen Feldzug gegen die Goten in Italien.